TO:
Trent,
enjoy

WANTED

Love ya bro.

Richard Coss
II Cor. 5:17

P.S. Met your brother
in NM.

The author preaching to an audience of 5,000 people at First Southern Baptist Church, Del City, Oklahoma, in 1980.

WANTED

RICHARD DAVID COSS

PELICAN PUBLISHING COMPANY
GRETNA 1999

First edition, 1975
First Pelican edition, 1989
Third printing, 1997
Second Pelican edition, 1999

ISBN 1-56554-688-1

Printed in the United States of America
Published by Pelican Publishing Company, Inc.
1000 Burmaster Street, Gretna, Louisiana 70053

To my constant traveling companion and co-laborer in the ministry of Jesus Christ, my sweetheart, Phyllis.

Also to:

Mike and Dee Story, Bob and Georgia Birdwell, Tim and Carol Vaughn, Dr. Sam Cornelius, J.B. Askins, Andy Cornelius, Harold Bittick, Shirley Hamilton, and Tim and Lenna Langley. We love you all.

And much thanks to Jo Ann Summers and Betty Howse for your help in editing the original manuscript.

Contents

Foreword

Richard Coss does not have a ministry. He is a ministry. His work for Christ is not a part of his life—it is his life. His every heartbeat is to help grow men and women into the likeness of Jesus Christ.

After his dramatic conversion in a federal penitentiary in 1969, he has been a flaming fire warming those who have been in sin's coldness. This book will warm your heart and lighten your path as you read the unfolding drama of a Saul who became a Paul. You will thrill at victory after victory from the dramatic life of Richard Coss.

Let me say as his pastor and close friend, that there is not one insincere bone in Richard Coss's body. He is true blue. He is genuine. He is solid for Christ. I am glad to know him and to be among the thousands in the lengthening shadow of his influence.

Dr. Bailey E. Smith
Past President
Southern Baptist Convention

INTRODUCTION

Richard David Coss is not an easy person to describe or to explain. My first experience with this young man was in an official capacity as United States Probation Officer for the Western District of Oklahoma. Richard was serving a sentence in the Federal Reformatory at El Reno, Oklahoma. He had an exceptional talent for winning friends and influencing people and did not hesitate to use this ability in trying to avoid harsh prison sentences when possible. However, this failed to work for him because he had committed other federal offenses while participating in the Work Release Program at the reformatory. Therefore, he was handed two substantial sentences in the United States District Court for the Western District of Oklahoma. At the time I thought justice had been served, and probably society was the greatest benefactor of the judge's decree.

Some time later, through the influence of the Christian Businessmen's Committee, Richard made a profession of faith in Christ. He became very active in witnessing and Bible study while still in prison. He proved himself worthy by institutional standards to participate again in the Work Release Program. During this time I became personally acquainted with him and involved with his Christian growth. On Sunday mornings I would pick Richard up at the Work Release Unit (outside the main confines of the reformatory) and take him with me to the First Baptist Church in

El Reno. Often, Richard would gather up several other fellow inmates and persuade them to join us in the worship service.

One hot summer night, I had made arrangements for Richard and several other inmates to attend the services of a tent crusade conducted by Larry Jones. On the way to town, Richard commented that he had lived so wholeheartedly for the Devil that he figured it was necessary to give equal time to the Lord. And he promised to give his testimony any time he was called upon to do so. Sure enough, Larry Jones, without advance notice, asked Richard to share his testimony that evening. Richard is already fiery and red-headed, with a ruddy complexion. But on this occasion, his color was even more heightened. He rose to his feet, giving a powerful testimony I shall not likely forget.

It has been my pleasure and duty since November 12, 1970, to supervise Richard for four years in my official capacity as United States Probation Officer. I have enjoyed his friendship and honesty. Even more, I have appreciated his faithfulness to the rules under which he must have and to the principles which he has chosen to follow. Not all stories are as successful as the one you will read in this book. Unfortunately, many professions of faith made behind prison walls are designed for the express purpose of obtaining individual freedom. Not so in the case of Richard David Coss.

CHARLES L. PIPPIN
U.S. Probation Officer

"God setteth the solitary in families:
he bringeth out those which are
bound with chains . . ."

(PSALMS 68:6)

WANTED

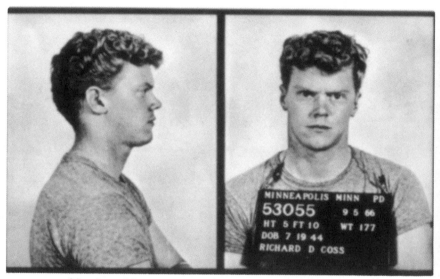

Mug shots of the author in 1966, following his arrest in Minneapolis.

CHAPTER 1

Caught

The stop light blinked red. As I waited for its signal to turn green, I had a funny feeling about the car coming up behind me. I watched the rear view mirror. Sure enough, my worst suspicions were confirmed. It was a squad car pulling up directly behind me! My heart pounded.

I was driving a stolen 1966 Chevy. Although I had put different license plates on it, I felt that those officers suspected something. Not only was the car hot, but I was hot! There were several warrants out for my arrest. Only the day before, in an argument, I had pulled a gun on a private detective. I threatened to shoot him and he ran—straight to the Minneapolis Police Department.

The light changed. I slowly turned left and drove a block to the next light. The police car followed me. I turned right and went another block. Again the police car turned behind me, still following me. I figured it was just a matter of time before the flashing lights and the siren came on and they pulled me over. I began to panic. It was time for action!

I dropped the Chevy into low gear. The torquing 396 engine screamed away from the corner with smoke belching from the fender wells. I quickly cut to a side street, then jammed the accelerator. Forty! Fifty! Sixty! Still they pursued. Seventy miles an hour! The squad car was in hot pursuit, but I knew I was pulling away from them. That 396 was a running machine.

I quickly glanced at the speedometer. I was now doing eighty miles an hour. The Chevy roared ahead. Suddenly I looked back to the edge of the road. I was horrified by what I saw! A lady was pushing a laundry cart full of clothes onto the street right in front of me. I laid on the horn and swerved to the left. She screamed and careened off the front of the car. Clothes went everywhere. Lucky for me it was only a cart I smashed and not the woman.

I kept on pushing that 396. The cops were still on my trail, but were falling back. I knew I must make some double turns and try to elude them, because by now other squad cars had probably been called into the chase. I slowed down enough to make a couple of quick turns and roared down another street. Dismayed and angered, I spotted another car falling in behind me.

Again I swerved onto another street. Then another, and another after that. I was desperate to evade my pursuers. Then, abruptly, the street ended at a T-shaped intersection in front of me. I tried to make the turn, but skidded on some gravel and sand left on the street from a construction job. My wheels lost traction. The car didn't turn. It kept going straight toward the bus stop across the street. Fortunately, the bench was unoccupied. My car crashed right through it and continued across the sidewalk, striking a utility pole.

I was knocked to the floorboard by the impact. Dazed, I sat up, taking a few seconds to regain my breath and my senses. The front of the car was caved in. Windshield glass was everywhere. I was in a real mess. I knew I had to get out of there.

Terrified, I jammed my hand into the glove compartment and fumbled for my pistol. My weapon was a wicked-looking .22 pistol with a 14-inch barrel. I grabbed it. The cylinder separated from the barrel. I frantically searched for it in the darkness.

Police cars were screeching to a halt all around me. I jumped out of the wreck and crouched behind the open door. The confrontation was beginning. In the darkness I tried desperately to get the cylinder into the gun frame. I just couldn't make it fit! Finally I thought I had it. I cocked the weapon, pointed it at the policeman closest to me, and squeezed the trigger.

Click! Nothing happened!

A shot whizzed through the air above my head, and the nearest cop yelled, "Throw down that gun!"

Too scared to think, I threw down the gun and took off running through the park directly behind me. Another shot rang out. This one was closer. The bullet whined right by my head and into the hedge beside me.

As I plunged through the bushes, I got my second wind. I could always run faster and longer when the police were chasing me than I could under ordinary circumstances. I could hear them shouting for me to stop, yelling to other officers to surround the park. But I continued my frantic escape attempt, running as fast as I could.

My luck held. I came to the other side of the park, darted across the street, and ran up a sidewalk in front of some tenement buildings. Then my luck ran out.

An old man who had observed the whole scene from his porch decided to play hero. He jumped out as I passed. He grabbed my arm. "Stop, you little punk!" he yelled.

Angrily, I jerked loose and shoved him down, but he had thwarted my hope of escape. I looked up to find a burly cop holding a billy club in his right hand and a .38 pistol in his left. "Okay, man, okay," I said, surrendering and throwing up my hands. "Don't shoot me. I quit."

The policeman wasn't satisfied with that. Evidently he wanted to even the score for all the trouble I'd given them that night. His billy club came hurtling down toward my head. Instinctively, I flung up my left arm as a shield. His club smashed against my elbow, leaving it numb. I thought my arm was broken.

"He's going to kill me," I thought. I grabbed wildly for his pistol, not really caring if I got shot, twisted it out of his hand, and threw it in the bushes. He grabbed me around the neck and struggled to hold me. I swung back with my right fist to his jaw and knocked him down. Suddenly I was sitting on top of him, slamming his face into the concrete sidewalk, cursing him every time I hit him.

Police swarmed all over me. A heavy shoe kicked me in the ribs. A pair of handcuffs slashed across my head. Another boot caught me in the back. A fist rammed me in the face. The rest of the squad had arrived!

I don't know how many times I was hit, but the next thing I knew I was chained and handcuffed and thrown into the back seat of a squad car. I looked at my hands. The handcuffs were cutting my wrists. They were so tight my hands were turning purple.

"Hey, man, how about loosening these cuffs?" I yelled when the officers finally got into the car.

"Shut up and keep quiet!" one of them shouted back.

That made me mad. I raised my foot over the back of his seat and kicked him in the head. He jumped around and slapped me across the face as hard as he could.

"You better cool it, Jake," his partner cautioned.

"Well, this punk kid had better shut up and settle down," he replied angrily.

I promised not to give him any more trouble if he'd just loosen those cuffs a little. Again I was commanded to shut my mouth. Furiously, I put both feet against the back of his seat, pushed with all my might and anger, and broke the hinges. They both cursed me then, but the officer driving the car told his partner to loosen the handcuffs. It was a small victory.

The ride to the station seemed to take forever. When we finally arrived, the booking sergeant took one look at me and said, "Take this guy to General Hospital immediately. I'm not booking him until he's had medical attention."

I must have really looked a sight! My shirt was torn. Blood was everywhere. My left arm ached when I tried to move it. My head was bleeding where the handcuffs had hit me. Both my eyes were black and blue and swollen nearly shut. My lips were split and bleeding.

The officers took me back to the squad car and drove me to the hospital. I created quite a sensation as I walked into the emergency room, both handcuffed and chained. I looked like a fugitive from a war!

A nurse ran over and took charge of me, ordering me to lie down on an examination table. A doctor came over and looked at me.

"What happened to you?" the doctor asked.

"I'm not sure," I mumbled. I really wasn't sure.

The next thing I knew, he was stitching up my head, and then he closed up an eyebrow with several stitches. He wound surgical tape around my back and ribs. He dressed the bruised elbow with an ace bandage and put it in a sling. After a few other little bandages were placed here and there, I was on my way back to the station to be booked.

I had been drinking when all this had happened, so I spent the first night in the "drunk tank." It was about midnight when the bars clanged shut behind me. As usual, the place was overflowing with weekend drunks.

I wasn't about to sleep on the floor, so I walked over to an old wino sleeping on a bench. I grabbed him by the shirt and threw him to the floor. He came to his feet cursing me.

"Find another bed," I ordered. "Can't you see I'm hurt? Mess with me and I'll kill you!"

He decided not to argue with me and went to sleep on the floor.

Spreading some newspapers on the filthy bench and using a roll of toilet paper for a pillow, I collapsed upon my makeshift bed and fell asleep.

About two hours later I was awakened by a hand rubbing up my leg. I slowly opened my eyes and squinted up into the smiling face of a man about forty years old. Sickened, I knew what he was: a jailhouse homosexual, a punk.

"Get the hell away from me!" I warned in no uncertain terms. To prove I meant it, I struck out with my foot, kicking him in the groin. He doubled up on the floor in pain. "You're a dead punk if you try that again!" I growled, then turned over and went back to sleep.

About six o'clock that morning the guard woke everyone up. He brought breakfast—a tin cup of coffee and a hard roll. I noticed everybody was staring at me.

There was a stainless steel mirror on the wall, so I painfully walked over to look at myself. No wonder they stared! My eyes were still purple. Dried blood matted my hair and eyebrows. My shirt was hanging in tatters. I was in some sad shape!

I hurt when I walked and I hurt when I talked. So I just kept to myself.

CHAPTER 2

Waiting in Jail

That day criminal charges were filed against me. I was transferred to the Hennepin County Jail to await trial. This jail didn't bother me much. I'd been in a lot of jails before. As a matter of fact, this was about my twenty-sixth arrest. Since I was only twenty-two years old, most of my time had already been spent behind bars. I found myself in a cell with a good mattress, so I settled down to do my county time until I went to court.

There's not a whole lot to do in a county jail except walk up and down the catwalk for exercise, do pushups in your cell, play cards, or just rap with other inmates. So I spent a lot of time reading. When you read anything in prison, you read it from cover to cover. You don't miss a thing. When I read magazines, I even read the advertisements. I enjoyed reading, which was a good thing because I had a strictly jailhouse education. I had dropped out of high school long before.

I seemed to retain a lot of the information I read, and I worked to acquire a large vocabulary. Often I wrote letters to Mom and Grandma, just to help pass the time. In fact, I became known as the guy who would read and write letters for the illiterate inmates.

I remember the day Indian Joe brought a letter to my cell for me to read to him. He had the cell right next to me and we were pretty good friends. He was a jolly guy a big heavy-set Sioux Indian from Minnesota. Joe was in jail on several hot check charges, plus a burglary charge. It looked like he was facing some time in the state penitentiary.

Scanning the contents of the letter, I glanced up at Indian Joe's eager face. I hesitated, not wanting to read it to him. "Joe, the news isn't good," I warned. The fact was, it was a "Dear John" letter I held in my hands.

"Read it anyhow," he instructed. So I did.

His wife was fed up with him, it said. She was taking the kids and leaving him. She never wanted to see him again. He was not to try to write or call her. He must forget she ever existed, the letter commanded. Then it was signed simply, "Goodbye. Your wife."

There was silence between us as Indian Joe stared at the floor. He reached out and took the letter from my hand, folded it, and put it in his shirt pocket. Then he quietly got up and walked next door to his cell. I didn't try to discuss it with him because I knew he wanted to be alone.

In the middle of the night I heard a loud crash or explosion. I wasn't sure which. Other inmates heard it too. Someone yelled, "Shut up that racket'" I didn't pay much attention to it, rolled over, and went back to sleep. If only I had known what was going on in the next cell.

Indian Joe had reached out through the bars at the top of his cell and managed, at arm's length, to unscrew a ceiling fluorescent light about two feet long. The explosion we heard was him breaking it in half on the bars. In extreme loneliness and desperation, feeling there was nothing left to live for since his wife and family had forsaken him, Indian Joe took the longest part of the jagged glass and began deliberately stabbing himself.

When he had severed many veins in his left arm, he changed hands and began to cut his right arm. Next, through the coveralls that he wore, he began to cut and scrape around his thighs and his legs. This was no cry for help. He really intended to kill himself, for his wounds were deep and they were numerous.

That morning I left my cell when they racked the doors and went over to wake up Indian Joe for breakfast. I thought it might help for him to have someone to talk to. When I looked through the barred window in his cell door, I saw him lying on his top bunk. There was an awful stench in the air. I opened the door and walked in. The fluorescent lightbulb was lying on the floor, caked with blood. Joe had bled so much during the night that his blood had soaked through the thin mattress from the top bunk and dripped down on the bottom bunk. Blood was on the ceiling and on every wall. The bloody toilet paper he had used to wipe his wounds was scattered all around. I thought he surely was dead.

"Joe! Joe!" I shook him. When he moaned slightly, I yelled for the guard. No one came. Quickly I told the other inmates what had happened, and we started beating on the bars with our cups to get the guards' attention. Finally, about fifteen minutes later, a guard came up to our catwalk, shouting, "What's the matter with you guys?"

"We've got a suicide attempt in here. He's nearly dead!"

The guard came alive. He ran to get help and to call a doctor.

Indian Joe had heard us call the guard. With what little strength he had left, he climbed down from his bunk, grabbed the broken bulb he used on himself, and held it as a weapon. When the guards attempted to enter his cell, he held them off with the jagged, bloody glass, swinging and stabbing at them. "Leave me alone," he cried out. "I want to die! Can't you understand? Just leave me alone." For several minutes he held off the guards. Then he began to sway. His knees buckled and he finally fainted from loss of blood.

The guards rushed in, picked up his unconscious body, and took him out on a stretcher. A trusty was sent to clean up his cell and change the mattress.

We wondered what would happen to the big Indian. We finally heard from the cell runner that Indian Joe had been taken to the hospital and patched up. That afternoon, as punishment for his "disorderly conduct," he was thrown into the hole—solitary confinement. Later that same evening a guard checked on Joe and found him hanging by his neck. He had taken some of the bandages off his wounds and made a noose. But again they got to him before he accomplished his goal. This time they stripped Joe of all his clothes, took off his bandages, and left him lying there on the cold, concrete floor. A guard was posted to watch him all the time, so he wouldn't try to take his life again.

Some folks would be horrified by Joe's story, but this kind of thing didn't bother me too much. I was already institutionalized: I had seen this sort of thing before. A great many horrors happen behind bars. There was one young man named Ronnie, only seventeen years old, who was mentally disturbed. He was a pyromaniac—he had a compulsion for starting fires. He'd been busted several times for setting fires in homes and restaurants, anywhere at all. Several of the older convicts had made a jailhouse punk out of him. In plain words, they raped him and made him a homosexual for their own pleasure.

Walking by Ronnie's cell one day, I saw that he had gotten hold of a razor blade somewhere, and was about to slash his wrists. I stepped into his cell. "What are you doing, Ronnie?"

"Man, life's just not worth living," he replied.

I talked him out of cutting his wrists and told him to ask for a transfer to another cell block. But he wouldn't do it because he feared for his life.

That county jail was no place for a seventeen-year-old boy. Ronnie was obviously mentally ill. He should have been under psychiatric care in a mental hospital. It's hard to understand why the authorities choose to place young men and other mentally ill cases in the county jails, thus exposing them to hardened criminals, sexual perverts, and unimagined terrors.

Four cells down from me was Hoss—so called because of his 6'5", 280-pound frame. Hoss had been sentenced to fifty years in prison for trying to sexually assault a nine-year-old girl. When she began to scream, he stabbed her to death. The child's mother came running to her rescue, and Hoss killed her too. It was hard for me to imagine. While he was in the county jail, Hoss was one of the quietest, nicest men there. Many times I'd go into his cell, trade a magazine or a candy bar, and talk for a while.

One day I got the nerve to ask, "Hoss, why'd you attack that little kid?"

He looked at me a minute, then sadly shook his head. "Man, I don't know why," he admitted slowly. "I was on drugs then. I guess I just flipped out."

After lights-out at night, the county jail changes drastically. There's no more chatter. It becomes a very lonely place as you lie there in your bunk, trying to go to sleep. You can't sleep because your mind is wandering out in the free world somewhere. You think how nice it is out there: no bars, no walls—free. Then you try to figure out how not to get caught next time, or how to beat your present rap.

Many times I asked myself, "Richard, what are you doing here? You're smarter than this. You have the ability to really do something good with your life!" I knew I did, and I knew I should. But it seemed like I never had the power to get loose from my old life. It was a trap I couldn't get out of. Oh, I could stay straight for maybe a week. Then I always got back on the bottle or started doing drugs again, which took away my desire to work, which meant I had to steal for money to operate, which ended up with me back in jail again. An old jailhouse saying is "What goes around comes around." God's Word says more plainly, "Your sins will find you out."

And they did—every time.

There was a homemade calendar on my cell wall. One morning I'd just finished scratching off the last day of four months when the guard came. "Richard David Coss," he shouted out. I knew it was time to go to court.

When I got there, I really attempted to put a story on the judge. I doubt if he believed me, but he ended up giving me probation— with a warning. He told me, "Richard, if I ever see you in my courtroom again, I'll sentence you under the habitual criminal act. You do understand what that means, don't you?"

"Yes, sir." I sure did. It carried from five years to life in the penitentiary. "Sir, you'll never see me back here again," I promised. "I'm going to go straight."

A few hours later I was dressed in my own clothes, given back my billfold, my watch, my ring, and my personal articles. I was free!

I did exactly what I told the judge I would do. I went straight—straight, that is, to the nearest liquor store. I bought a bottle of vodka, went to a buddy's apartment, got drunk, and planned my next score.

CHAPTER 3

Growing Up
on a Barstool

People often ask me, "Richard, how in the world did you get to be that way?"

From early childhood I was destined to live a rough life. My mother and dad operated beer joints and honky tonks ever since I can remember. By the time I was five years old, I could swear up and down and repeat the dirty jokes with the rest of the barroom crowd.

I literally grew up on a barstool. There was never a backyard for me to play in, no swing set, no trees to climb. No brother or sister or playmates. My playground was the bar where my mom and dad worked. What a life for a child!

My parents patronized other taverns quite a bit when they were off their regular job. I was carted around with them from joint to joint. The owner of one place they frequented felt so sorry for me that he bought me a tricycle. I thought it was great fun wheeling around the pool tables and the bar.

There was never much love in our home. My mom and dad were always flying at each other's throats, and it seemed like I was caught in between. Soon I began to lose interest in my home— then school and friends. I committed my first crime about this time. I was nine years old. A friend of mine was hungry and didn't have money for food, so I stole several bags of groceries from a car for him.

By the time I was eleven, I refused to obey anyone who had any authority over me. One day my school teacher corrected me about my misconduct. "Go to hell!" I spat defiantly. It flew all over her, and she slapped me in the face. Without blinking, I slapped her back. Inwardly I was crying, "Please, please, won't somebody love me? Won't somebody please listen to me, notice me, believe in me?"

The only sure way I knew to get attention was to make trouble. Then I got plenty of attention—from the police, the juvenile authorities, the judges, and my school principal. I was always in trouble. Finally, all these people gave up on me, and a judge sent me to the State Training School for Boys in Waukesha, Wisconsin. I was twelve years old.

My first encounter with reform school taught me that it was simply a school for criminals. I sat captivated, fascinated, listening to the older boys' stories about stealing cars, writing hot checks, and conning people. They taught me how to be a better liar, and a better cheater. And I quickly learned that if I didn't stand up and fight for my rights, the other guys would bully me all the time. For example, there was an initiation time for me there in reform school. It was called a blanket party. One night a couple of fellows sneaked up behind me, threw an army blanket over my head, and held me while half a dozen fists flailed away at me. They kicked me and left me where I fell to the floor. I knew who one of the boys was, and I waited for my chance to get back at him. When I caught him coming in the door to our cottage alone the next day, I tore into him. After I had really whipped him, I gave him a message for the others: If his buddies didn't leave me alone, the rest of them were going to get the same treatment, one by one, until I evened the score. After that, no one messed around with me or picked on me—not even the bigger guys. They seemed to respect someone who stood on his own two feet and slugged it out.

I remembered my father's advice to me just before I left for reform school. "Son", he said, "don't ever let anybody step on your toes. If you want anything good out of life, you've gotta fight for it." I figured dad knew what he was talking about. He was a big guy, a Marine Corps veteran, and he had been a weight lifter and a boxer. I wanted to be like him, so I took his advice to heart. "You've gotta fight for what you want." So I learned to be a fighter, and I learned how to con people. I was on my way to bigger and better things.

Even here I was always in trouble. For instance, a person couldn't smoke unless he was sixteen and had permission from his parents. I wasn't and didn't, so I was always getting busted for smoking. For each infraction of the rules, they'd write me up, and after the third time I had to go to court and then be sent to detention cottage. That's where I spent twelve of my eighteen months—in detention cottage.

What was detention cottage? A place of hard labor run by the biggest, meanest officers in the place. There were always about twenty of us in detention cottage. And the guards were tough on us. Every day we worked hard. We would be sent out to mow the grounds with push mowers that had the wheels tightened so much they would hardly turn. A guy really had to push hard to keep up with the rest of the fellows and get the job done, or else there would be more severe punishment.

They used to send us out with crosscut saws and axes to cut down any big, dead, or diseased trees. After the tree was felled, we'd have to dig around its stump and chop all the roots loose, leaving the stump completely free. Then we'd dig a huge hole right next to it, roll the stump into the hole, and cover it up. Finally, we had to split and stack all the wood from the fallen tree.

There was also the rock pile. For more severe punishment, we had to go over to the rock pile, fill gunnysacks with rocks just heavy enough that we couldn't lift them. We had to drag them about a hundred yards, dump them and restack the pile of rocks. That pile of rocks which was about ten feet wide and ten feet tall, was moved all over the grounds. Three or four fellows were working on the rock pile just about every day. I used up many gunnysacks moving that rock pile around.

After suppertime in detention cottage we had to sit still until ten o'clock. We sat straight in our chairs, our feet flat on the floor, our arms folded in front of us, our eyes on the American flag straight ahead. We couldn't take our eyes off the flag. We couldn't move. We couldn't do anything unless it was urgent. An officer sat at his desk in front of the flag, doing his paperwork. We'd always try to sneak smokes or whisper, but the old guard was a little quicker than we were. He'd always catch us and make us wax the floor!

Detention cottage had a big marble floor. For breaking silence, we had to get down on our hands and knees and wax it. Then we had to buff it with an old army blanket. Every night somebody had to buff that marble floor. I believe it was the smoothest floor in the state! It wouldn't have been so bad, except that we were required to wear nightgowns. When we knelt down on our knees the nightgowns always came up above our knees. After about half an hour on the hard marble, big, round blisters the size of half dollars rose up on our knees. That wasn't fun. It really hurt. But that was the price we paid for misbehaving in detention cottage.

Once I instigated a riot in our regular cottage. My job was to switch out the lights that evening when the officer wasn't looking so the riot could take place in the darkness. Then the guard wouldn't know who to blame. At the set time I flipped the switch—and all hell broke loose. Chairs were hurled through the air. We smashed the television set and the radio. We tore apart the furniture and shattered the windows. The guard caught it from all sides and was hurt rather badly. It didn't take the officials long to find out who the instigator was, and I was sent back to detention cottage again. Back to the rock pile and that shining marble floor.

I was really getting sick of reform school. Once I tried to run away, but I was caught and brought back. I wanted out so much that I decided to straighten up. I quit smoking cigarettes. I started saying "Yes sir" and "No sir" to the guards. I started following the rules and regulations they held so sacred, instead of bucking them. I quit sassing the officers. I went back to school, tried to apply myself, and got some pretty good grades. I hadn't really had a change of heart. I just wanted out! I was willing to do anything I had to do to be free again.

Finally, several months later, I was released. I was put on a train headed for Minneapolis. My mom and dad had moved there from Webster, Wisconsin while I was in reform school. They were working in a liquor store on Franklin Avenue.

My dad met me at the train depot. I hugged him because it was good to see him again. In the year and a half I'd been away in reform school, my parents only came to see me once. I think it had been to break the monotony of loneliness that I'd stayed in trouble so much there.

Dad took me out to eat. Then we shopped for some new street clothes, because the only clothing I had that would fit me was the institutional garb given me at the reform school. I wouldn't be caught dead in them now—I was free! So I got some new clothes, some new personal articles, and a new lease on life. Then I went to my new home to see my mother.

It was a different location, but I found myself back in the same type of environment I had left a year and a half earlier: beer joints, honky tonks, nightclubs. My folks weren't getting along any better than before. It was all the same—the same old problems, the same old life. There I was again. Home, sweet home.

The author at age seven.

The author at age 22 doing hard time in El Reno Prison.

CHAPTER 4

On the Streets

I soon discovered that of the hundreds of neighborhoods there are in the Twin Cities, my parents had chosen to live in the roughest one of all. The area of Fourteenth Street and Franklin in South Minneapolis was lined with liquor stores, bars, nightclubs, honky tonks, "flesh flick" theaters, strip joints, pool halls, and pawn shops. Junk yards and scrap iron places surrounded us. Real classy neighborhood. Talk about living on the other side of the tracks!

Several neighborhood gangs continually roamed the streets. One day I was on my way up Fourteenth Street to a movie. I walked by a house that had about twenty teenagers sitting on the porch. One of the girls called out, "Hey, look at old Carrot Top slinkin' by!" They all laughed.

I didn't like people making fun of my red hair. I stopped, turned, and walked over to the group. They sat silently watching me. In a deadly voice I told the girl, "If you've got something to say to me, I suggest you say it to my face. I get real upset with people who talk about me behind my back."

"Look man, I didn't mean nothin'," she apologized.

"Leave her alone, man," the girl's boyfriend told me.

I kept up my bluff. "Listen," I snapped, "I just got back from reform school, and I really don't care much what happens now. If you're looking for a fight, you picked the right guy."

I soon began getting involved with one of the roughest gangs in

33

that part of the city, the Fourteenth Street Gang. We had from twenty-five to thirty members at any given time. That was back in the late fifties, the "hoodlum" days. All of our gang members wore black leather jackets and had long hair slicked back in a ducktail. Many of us carried switchblades and dog chains—weapons of defense to use on rival gangs.

Our gang literally ruled the neighborhood. We stole and fought and partied nearly every night. We were constantly in trouble, and most of us were kicked out of school. As a fifteen-year-old boy I was expelled from school. I never went back. (I finished my high school education in a federal prison when I was twenty-four.) Also at the age of fifteen I found myself the youngest person in the state of Minnesota ever to be sent to the Hennepin County Work Farm, better known as "Parker's Lake Resort." I had been arrested for driving without a license and driving while intoxicated several times, so I was finally sentenced to thirty days in the county work farm. It made headlines in the newspaper. That's some way to make the news!

I argued with the judge. "Hey, man, Your Honor, you can't send me out there. I'm only fifteen years old, see. I'm a juvenile."

That old judge gravely replied, "Young man, just watch me and see what I can and can't do." And off I went to the work farm for thirty days.

I didn't realize it at the time, but I was going to spend many, many more months in that county prison farm. After that first thirty days, I later had to serve another sixty. When I was sixteen, I served ninety. Just before I turned seventeen, I served 120 days for DWI. I really had something to brag about to my gang members. I was in trouble all the time. Most of the kids looked up to me. I was building quite a reputation for myself in our neighborhood. Fighting, drinking, stealing, and being busted. But every time I served another sentence, I came out more of a hero in my neighborhood.

About ten of our gang members were girls. They were constantly in trouble. All of us had miserable home lives. Most of our parents had drinking problems, or were splitting up, or were fighting all the time. The same old patterns seemed to be repeating the cycle in our lives, but we didn't stop to look at what was happening.

There were several churches in our neighborhood, but they never touched us. Not one person ever stopped to tell us about Jesus Christ and His better way of life. No one ever came to invite us to a revival. They just rolled up their windows tightly, locked their doors, and passed us by on their way to their nice, stained glass sanctuaries. We often sat on the porch steps watching them go by in their fine suits and fancy dresses, driving their new cars. They were evidently too busy to waste time on us black leather-jacketed hoodlums. Perhaps they thought we weren't worth saving. Maybe they thought Christ didn't die for us, that Christianity was merely for good folks like them. Most likely they were just afraid of us.

I started floating checks when I was sixteen. I was hitting the bottle heavily, nearly an alcoholic. There was a booze party nearly every night. At one of these parties I met a friend I would spend much time with. His name was George Harmon.

As a child, George had polio, which left him crippled. He had walked with crutches since he was a little boy. From his waist up he was built like Hercules, very muscular, very strong. There wasn't anybody in town he couldn't whip. Often he'd get in the first lick of a fight with his crutch, because he used his crutches as weapons.

Many times George and I would team up and go to the "queer parks" in downtown Minneapolis. We'd let a homosexual pick us up, and we'd walk with him over into the shadowy darkness of the park. Then, when he least expected it, we'd jump him, knock him to the ground, kick him a few times, and take everything he had of any value—his ring, his watch, his billfold. We'd leave him lying there bleeding and crying, and we'd walk away laughing like it was a big joke. We knew he wouldn't turn us in because the police didn't like "queers" any better than hoodlums. Usually the police themselves would hassle homosexuals whenever they tried to make a complaint. So we did this whenever we felt like doing it, without fear of getting in trouble.

George and I pulled off a lot of burglaries and thefts together. Whenever there was an eyewitness to identify us, George was always picked up. The police knew there wasn't anybody else in town who walked on crutches as mean as George was. He would always get thirty, sixty, ninety days, or even six months in the workhouse or the county jail. They never sent George to prison back then. They probably felt sorry for him because he was crippled and had no parents. He lived with his grandmother. Whatever the reason, George always seemed to get light sentences. And he never implicated me. The police would always grill him: "Come on, George. Tell us who the red-headed guy with you was. Cooperate with us and make it easy on yourself."

"Man, you're talking to the wrong guy," he'd reply. "I'm no snitch." George never did cop out.

Sometimes when I got busted on my own and thrown into the tank, I'd find George already there. We'd take over our tank and run it. If anybody gave us any lip, we'd jump him and bust his head with a fist or a crutch. We were quite a pair.

Late one evening George, his pregnant girlfriend, and I were walking down Franklin Avenue. A big fellow about forty years old drunkenly stumbled out of a doorway as we passed. He bumped into George's girlfriend and lurched right on by without a word.

"Hey, man, get yourself back here," George yelled at him.

The fellow probably figured we were just a couple of teenage punks he could take care of in short order. He turned to George. "You talking to me, kid?"

"Yes, I am," George politely told him. "You almost knocked my friend over. I want you to apologize to her."

The man spouted out a string of profanities and turned on his heel to leave. Suddenly a crutch came smashing down across his head. He crumpled to the sidewalk. Blood poured out from the side of his face. He didn't move. He never knew what hit him. And we never knew whether he lived or died. We just kept walking.

CHAPTER 5

My Fighting Fists

Even though I did not deserve it, I realize now that God was watching over me in those days. I always chalked everything up to my being "lucky." I'd start a bar fight at the bat of an eye. I always threw the first punch as hard as I could so I wouldn't have too many more jabs to follow. The fights never lasted long and I almost always won. But it seemed like whoever was with me those times usually got hurt—stabbed or beaten or kicked or cracked with a pool cue. It finally got to where a lot of my friends wouldn't go anywhere with me because of the bad reputation of my fighting fists.

After the sidewalk episode, George Harmon moved out of my neighborhood and laid low for awhile. Since he was gone, I started running around with Howie. Howie and I were good drinking buddies. He was a big guy who could hold his own in a fight. Nearly every week Howie and I managed to get into some pretty tough scrapes.

One snowy night in Minneapolis we dropped into a particular bar where we drank several pitchers of beer. We were feeling no pain when the bartender announced, "Sorry, fellows, but you're gonna have to leave. This here bar's been rented by some sailors for a private party and it's time for it to start."

So we got ready to leave. About that time several of the sailors came in. One of them noticed Howie and me still sitting in a booth. He stepped quickly over to us and said, "This is a private party. You guys get out."

I stood up like I was leaving. The sailor was wide open, taking off his Navy peacoat just then, so I caught him with a hard right cross. He doubled up and hit the floor. I let the others know that I would only leave when I got good and ready.

Then the other sailors jumped into the fight. I just wound up with some bruised knuckles. But poor old Howie! One of the sailors busted a large pitcher of beer and rammed the jagged glass edges through Howie's hand. Another one hit him across the back with a pool cue. I finished off one guy with the big end of a pool cue and another one with a foot to the groin.

We figured we'd better split. Howie hit the front door and I fled out the back door, both as fast as we could go. But, wouldn't you know it, Howie ran right into two policemen. Off he went to the jailhouse while I managed to escape.

I really don't know why I always frequented the sleaziest joints. One night I was hunting for a fellow named Wally who had burned me in a drug deal. After searching through several places, I found him in a bar called the Snake Pit. That was a good name for it, because that's about what it was—a snake pit. I pulled up a stool beside Wally. When he looked at me, I knew he was a little scared of me.

"Want a beer?" he asked.

"Sure, I'll drink a beer with you."

As we sat there drinking, suddenly an old man about three bar stools down from us fell off his perch, hitting the floor with a thud. I went over, picked him up, dusted him off, and propped him back up on his bar stool. "Thanks," he mumbled. I thought the old man was drunk. He must have been seventy years old. He sat there shaking his head as he drank a couple more beers. Then he fell again. This time he didn't get up. He was dead of a heart attack.

It took half an hour for the ambulance to get there. The old man's body was right in the pathway to the jukebox. Nobody wanted to drag him out of the way. People just stepped over him, chose their favorite hits, and continued dancing, laughing, joking. Finally the police and the ambulance came to cart away the body. Things settled down some, but not enough to talk seriously.

I maneuvered Wally into stepping out back with me. I told him we had to talk about an important deal. Well, like a big old duck, he waddled out the door first. When he turned around, I was ready for him. I hit him as hard as I could, right between the eyes. He had a cigarette between his lips, and it fell inside his mouth as he dropped to the ground on his back. The punch knocked him out cold. But he lay there twitching, his tongue darting in and out of his mouth because the cigarette was burning inside of his mouth.

A waitress ran out to see what had happened. She saw him lying there with blood coming out one ear and running out his nose. Smoke was curling out of his mouth. "Do something!" she screamed at me. "Do something, quick!"

"Back off, lady," I commanded. "I'll do something." I was wearing heavy combat boots. I hauled off and kicked him in the head as hard as I could. The cigarette butt flew out of his mouth. I walked off. My responsibility was over.

Several days later I was arrested for assault and battery. I had to wait about thirty days in the jailhouse before I went to court, because the man's condition was so grave that the doctors weren't sure whether he would live or die. I nearly had a manslaughter case on my head. Finally he pulled through, so the judge let me go with my thirty days county jail time. Old Wally had learned his lesson though. He never burned me again.

Bobby was another friend of mine who was quite a fighter. He claimed to know some karate, which he used on a few drunks that we rolled. One night as we were walking down Portland Avenue, we saw two dudes go by in a car. They hollered at us, so we yelled back and shot them the finger. They slammed on their brakes and jumped out of the car. Bobby and I had no weapons at all with us. Here these two dudes came. One of them pulled a knife and began slashing at Bobby. I was down on the ground wrestling the other fellow. I finally got loose of him, kicking him a couple of times. I saw that the boy with the knife was working Bobby over.

"Don't worry, Bobby, I'll get him," I yelled. "I've got my switch-blade."

They didn't stop to notice that I really didn't have a knife. What I said must have scared them though, because they both got up and ran. I drove Bobby to General Hospital. Luckily, he wasn't hurt badly. His wounds were superficial and easily closed with a few stitches. The doctors released him after a few hours.

Two nights later Bobby and I threw big party at my apartment. There were thirty-five or forty teenagers milling around the apartment, drinking, laughing. Suddenly five Indian boys walked in. They were known all around as party crashers.

"You can stay as long as you don't cause any trouble," I told them. "No trouble—understand?"

"Sure, baby," they laughed. "Want to smoke the peacepipe?"

Right away one of them started hustling my girlfriend. That was too much for me. I jerked his arm away. "Let's go, man. Just you and me, down the back stairs, out to the alley. Let's settle this."

He gladly started down the back stairs. I followed him, not realizing there were four other Indians softly coming after me. Before the little guy ahead of me knew what happened, I laid into him. He hit the ground and got right back up. I hit him again. Again he went down. He was a real scrapper. He'd come out swinging, but he was smaller than I. I had a lot of reach on him, plus about forty pounds. Every time I hit him, he went down. Just before I finished him off, I realized I was surrounded by his four friends.

What now? I was no match for five. Then old Bobby showed up, and the odds were suddenly much better. I knew he was still hurting from his knife wounds, but I needed the help. Bobby had a beer bottle in his hand that he busted over the handrail on the stairs. The fight was on!

I finally managed to put the little boy down for good and grabbed another one. I was trying to work my way over to Bobby because he had three on him. Suddenly a bottle crashed across

Bobby's head, and he dropped to the ground. I grabbed a two-by-four lying in the alley and started swinging wildly, yelling at the top of my lungs. When I was drunk and mad, I would go crazy. I was a wild man. I had the strength of every demon in hell. The Indian guys finally ran. I helped Bobby back up to my place and then back to General Hospital for more stitches. He kept muttering, "Never again, man, never again." Poor Bobby. He wouldn't go out with me any more, and he never came back to my parties.

One Friday afternoon on the first of the month, my friend T-Boy came by. He wanted me to go out with him that evening.

"Listen, Richard," he confided, "I know this old man who gets his $265 pension check the first of every month. He cashes it at Annie's Bar and Grill, has a couple of drinks, and walks home with the cash in his pocket. So we can get two hundred and sixty-five easy bucks—just like that!" He snapped his fingers.

"Sounds like a simple score, man," I agreed. "I'll meet you there."

We arranged the time and place to meet. It was down Franklin Avenue in our neighborhood. "By the way," T-Boy mentioned, "my cousin, Jeanie, is goin', with us."

"No problem."

We decided to use her to get the old man's attention while one of us knocked him in the head. But once again God intervened in my life when I didn't even know it. Something else came up, so I decided not to go with T-Boy and Jeanie.

They went out together to roll the old man. T-Boy was smart enough to talk Jeanie into hitting the old man. She put all she had into the swing, and she slammed him across the head with a two-by-four. The old man died instantly.

Both T-Boy and Jeanie got long prison terms. When I read about it in the papers and heard it on the news, man, was I glad I hadn't gone along with them. If I had, I knew I would have been given fifteen or twenty years in the Minnesota State Penitentiary. The last I heard, Jeanie is still there today.

So many times I came close to killing somebody or having a part in someone's death. During a party one night I picked the drunkest person of all, "Little Earl," to go get the food. Earl was everybody's buddy, simply because he was over twenty-one and could buy booze. He could drink more alcohol than several of us put together. Already this evening he had put away a pint of vodka and several cans of beer. He was really loaded.

I decided it would be a good trick to pull on Earl to send him down to McDonald's for hamburgers. He was so drunk we all knew he'd never make it. He was bound to have an accident on the way. I told everybody what I was going to do. They laughed. What a big joke.

Earl usually had money on him, so he agreed to go. It was about eleven o'clock at night when Earl staggered to his car. A '57 Lincoln, it had the dual slanted headlights with the point above them molded into the metal fender—a deadly weapon. Earl took off down Portland Avenue. In his drunkenness, he didn't even see the woman in front of him. She was crossing in the middle of the street rather than at the street light. He was going forty-five miles an hour when he hit her. As the point of that fender above the headlight caught the woman in the stomach, it literally cut her in half. She died instantly.

Immediately, Earl opened the pack of cigarettes he had in his pocket. He chewed up the tobacco in his mouth, even swallowing some of it, and spitting some out. The tobacco covered up the alcohol smell. Since Earl had drunk mostly vodka, the police did not detect that he was DWI that evening. Besides, he had sobered up quickly when he realized what happened.

When the police came, he just faked a sickness over hitting the woman. Earl lost his driver's license because he had been speeding, and they fined him for negligent driving.

But I knew it was murder. And I was a part of that murder. It had been my idea of a joke on Earl. Some joke!

CHAPTER 6

Wheeling and Dealing to Mexico

At this time in my life I thought that money was the answer for everything. It seemed I had always been unhappy. I still was. So I came to the conclusion that if I could buy all the things I really wanted—a nice car, great apartment, fine clothes—I would finally be content. I had tried so hard and searched so long for happiness in many different ways, never really finding it. I thought surely enough money could buy happiness for me.

Oh, there had been exciting times in my adventures. The Bible says that sin is fun for a while, and I'd had fun at times. It was fun to get drunk. It was fun to win a fight. It was exciting to steal. But it was no fun sitting in the back seat of a squad car headed for the county jail, nor hearing the judge say, "Ninety days, Richard." The Word of God is right on. In Hebrews 11:25 it says that Moses chose rather to suffer affliction with the people of God than to enjoy the fleeting pleasures of sin. Sin is fun only for a short while. It never brings lasting joy or peace. It promises happiness, but leaves emptiness.

So I turned to monetary gain for my pleasure. There was just one catch: I didn't want to work for money. The only other way for me to get it was to steal. And I wanted money in large quantities. So I figured out a way.

I had owned enough cars in the state of Minnesota to know that Minnesota was a "non-title" state. With simply a blank Minnesota transfer card I could sell a car without a title by using the excuse that the title had been sent to the capital and had not yet come back in the mail. I discovered there was easy money to be had in this setup. I began to steal cars.

I stole them on the north side of Minneapolis and sold them on the south side. Or I stole them on the south side to sell on the north side. I stole them on the east side of Minneapolis and sold them over in St. Paul, or from St. Paul to Bloomington. I stole and sold cars for four months.

I nearly drove the car dealers batty. They put a private detective on my heels, trying to find me. I never gave them my name, but they had my description: five feet eleven, red hair, blue eyes, about 185 pounds. The way I stole all the cars was from car dealers. I figured they had burned enough people anyway, so it would serve them right to get burned a little themselves. I knew that if they let me test drive a car by myself and I didn't return, the police wouldn't handle the case as a stolen car for thirty days. So, for the first month or two, I had a great time! Even if the police were watching for me, they didn't have any warrants out for my arrest.

Right away, I set myself up as a car jockey. I even had some cards printed up: "Joe Dawson, Fine Used Cars." One of my stories went this way. "Listen friend, I've just picked up this car at the auto auction and I'd like to make about $150 on it." I was a good con man. It seemed I could put any story over on anybody I wanted and get them to believe it. I stole from car dealers and sold to car dealers. No wonder the dealers were going crazy.

After four months of this, I had managed to get most of the things I had wanted. A Dodge Polara convertible. Two nice, furnished apartments. All the sharp clothes I could wear. The color television and the stereo, with all the records. Parties every night at my apartment, turning everybody on with narcotic cough medicines. I had traded the booze kick for drinking codeine, but I still kept my cabinets full of booze for those who wanted alcohol. Big man, big parties, big fun—but it never lasted. I still wasn't happy.

Deciding that happiness must be found in a geographical location, I began to travel. I went to Omaha and to Albuquerque. Then to Corpus Christi, Galveston, and Houston. Along the way I pulled off a few scores for some extra traveling money. I went over to New Orleans for a while. Yet my life was so empty. I thought I was lonely for my friends, so I returned to Minneapolis. That was a mistake.

The cops were ready for me. Soon after I returned, I stole and sold a few more cars. It was during this time that I was driving the 396 Chevy I wrecked in the high-speed chase described in the opening chapter. The police beat me so severely they had to take me to the hospital before booking me. Then I was booked into the county jail.

The authorities had me down for thirty-one stolen cars. The State of Minnesota's title department was quite upset with me. They had been trying to install a computerized system for title cataloging when all of these hot titles came through and they weren't detected right away. Others the machine would just spit back out. I really had the title department going in circles for awhile.

The authorities threatened to charge me with all thirty-one counts, but in the end they just charged me with one. I really attempted to put my story over on the case worker and the judge. Once again I got off lucky—with probation.

It was in the middle of winter when I again found myself thinking about leaving Minneapolis to head south. I talked an Indian buddy of mine, a heist man named Scotty, into going with me. We took off for El Paso, Texas, stopping to steal a couple of cars along the way. By the time we reached El Paso, we were so broke we only had enough money to stay at a sleazy, ratty, little hotel. I say it was ratty because we saw a few of the varmints in our room every night. But it was cheap rent.

Immediately we made several contacts across the border in Juarez with people we could sell hot cars to. Our contact wanted four-door models, any year. He said he could buy them and resell them for taxicabs, either there in Juarez or in the interior of Mexico. Evidently they were a pretty hot item down there, since he said he could sell all the four-doors we could bring them.

We made an appointment with the contact. At the proper time we drove our cars across the border. He wasn't there. We waited about half an hour. Still our man didn't show. Being in a strange country, not knowing the language, we began to get a little jumpy. Rightly so. All at once two men dressed in suits came around the corner. I smelled "cop" and began to run. It was too late. A voice yelled, "Stop or we shoot you." I stopped. When I turned to look, I saw a .45 pointing right at my head.

They flashed their badges at us and pushed us back around the corner to the back seat of a '59 Buick. One man kept the gun pointed at us while the other drove. I did some quick thinking. "This is 1967. How come they're driving a '59 Buick? Maybe they aren't policemen at all. Yea, that's it! They're rippin' us off. They're going to hijack us, take us out in the country, and dump us. Maybe even shoot us! Then they'll go back and get our car."

Suddenly, I had to know the truth. "Let me see your badge again, officer," I demanded of the one holding the gun. However, he didn't understand a word I said. I turned to the other. "Tell him I want to see that ID again."

The driver quickly translated my request. I was handed the badge. As I examined it I was oddly relieved. Sure enough, they were policemen. They belonged to the Servicito Secreta de Mexico, the Mexican Secret Service. At least I knew what I was up against. I figured my chances with them were a lot better than being shanghaied by a couple of Mexican bandits.

That Servicito Secreta de Mexico was some top-class organization, though. Their '59 Buick was barely running. Their suits had frayed cuffs and necks and their shirts were old and tattered. They both looked like a couple of Al Capone's hit men. They really didn't seem to have a whole lot going for them.

They drove us right to the Chihuahua Prison in Juarez, where we were fingerprinted, interrogated, and had some mug shots made. Then we were brought before the captain of the guards.

"Lay your billfolds out here with your rings and watches on the table," he commanded. "Also, take off your belts." A cop hung our belts on a great big rack holding about seventy other belts. I noticed that our two happened to be good leather belts, the nicest ones on the rack. And down inside I realized that they wouldn't be hanging there very long.

The captain of the guards then pulled out a large manilla envelope and put our things into it. "Upon your release these articles will be returned to you," he assured us as he sealed the envelope and wrote our names on it. I saw no reason not to believe him. I didn't know that about an hour later our rings and watches would be down on the market going to some traveler or tourist for the highest bid.

Scotty and I were thrown into the hole at the Chihuahua Prison. I had been in a lot of solitary confinement cells before and a lot of holes, but this one hit a new low. The room, about six by sixteen, held twenty-one of us. There was one commode in it, and a pipe sticking through the wall was called a shower. It had no faucet. Ice cold water came streaming out in about a one-inch flow.

Scotty, was a big six-foot-six Indian. Fortunately, he was the meanest looking guy in the hole. That was one reason I liked having him for a partner, because not too many people messed around with us when they got a good look at him. They never knew that if poor old Scotty didn't have a gun he was afraid of his own shadow.

There were nineteen Mexican inmates with us in that tank. They couldn't speak English. We couldn't speak Spanish. So not a whole lot was said, although we tried to converse a little. They were friendly enough to us. We soon discovered that we were to get only two meals a day. And you could hardly call those meals—beans twice a day with one cup of coffee. I didn't know how long we could take this kind of treatment. We had to stay eight days in the hole. I came down with dysentery, but Scotty managed to stay healthy.

Finally, we were transferred out into the main yard of the

penitentiary. That was one of the wildest, meanest places I have ever been in my life. But most of the inmates there had it easier than they did out in the free world. They got their two meals of beans a day and weren't required to do much. Of the thousand inmates, only about a dozen worked. They were cooks, who didn't strain themselves preparing beans every meal. Once a day they would fix "jatole" to go with the beans. Jatole is a watered down cornmeal mush. Scotty once remarked "This junk would gag a maggot on a gut wagon." His observation made it even harder to eat. The only way I could choke the stuff down was to pour about a cupful of sugar into the coffee can (there were no bowls) with the jatole in it. Everybody had one spoon. Man, this was a new experience for me.

Inside the walls there were fifteen quonset-like huts. As we walked around the yard, I looked up and counted six gun towers high upon the surrounding adobe walls. The guards always carried their guns on them. They didn't bother us much, because they knew the American Consul would be coming to visit us right away.

We were assigned to hut number eleven, along with about 40 other inmates. Our quarters had a dirt floor, one stool, one shower, no hot water. There was a four-burner gas stove in the middle of the room. When we walked in, several Mexicans greeted Scotty and I, offering us a little assistance. In their broken English and with much gesturing, they conveyed the idea that we should spray ourselves every evening before retiring with some type of fuel oil. This was necessary, they indicated, to keep the "chin-chis" off us. Chin-chis were little bedbugs that crawled all over the place. Everybody in the hut smelled like fuel oil, but it was the only thing we could do to keep the bugs from eating us up at night. Scotty and I managed to get one blanket each, and we slept on a piece of cardboard at night. We didn't take our shoes off, nor our socks. We left our clothes on all the time, except when we showered during the day.

There was a pipe running from the main wall that came out a

hole in our wall. The cold water ran from it down into a series of concrete wash basins. As one basin filled up, the water would overflow into another one, then another as it kept going downhill. The wash basins had concrete scrubboards built into them. This was where we washed our clothes. Every Monday morning we were handed a bar of lye soap to do our laundry with. We would scrub out clothes, rinse them, and then hang them up to dry. We knew if we turned our heads, our clothes would be gone. There were a thousand thieves in that penitentiary after every piece of clothing we owned. Some of the inmates would even go so far as to stab another for a decent pair of shoes or a warm sweater or jacket.

Even in Juarez it gets quite cold at night in February. Since I was pretty sick with dysentery by this time, I was really feeling miserable. The daily supply of beans didn't help. Finally, a nurse was called in for me. She gave me a shot of something that cured my dysentery. A couple of days later I was feeling more like my old self.

In the fifty-five days Scotty and I spent in the Juarez prison, there were four brutal murders. All four were over narcotics. It seemed like each inmate carried a syringe in one back pocket and a knife in the other. It was quite a place. I was a drug user before, but down there I had no desire to get into that scene. I was still a stranger, and I didn't know what I might let myself in for.

Scotty and I stuck pretty close together. As a matter of fact, we never left each other's sight. We always watched out for each other's back. Several times we were threatened with our lives for some of our clothing. But we never gave in to them. Then they offered to trade us drugs for our clothing, but that was no deal either. When they saw we meant to keep what we had, they finally stopped the threats. After that, we were pretty much left alone.

When we had been there a few weeks, we learned to speak a little Spanish. We made some new friends, fellows from the interior of Mexico who had been busted on crimes in Chihuahua and sent to prison here. The time passed a lot faster as we talked with these fellows and played cards or shot dice with them.

Once we asked the American Consul for some decent maga-

zines to read to pass the time. He brought us some 1940 *Readers'*
Digests and some 1939-40 *Look, Post,* and *Life* magazines. "Sorry,
fellows," he told us, "but this is all I have available for you. I hope
you like history."

The homosexual ratio there in the Juarez prison was virtually
nonexistent. I only saw one homosexual out of a thousand
inmates. There was a reason: for $1.80 an inmate could have a
prostitute come in to visit on Thursday or Sunday. Or a wife or a
girlfriend could come in and spend the day. The inmates could
sleep with them if they had a private place to go. Some of them
didn't care whether they had a private place or not. Although it
was quite loose down there, there was no homosexual problem as
in the United States prisons, where it is sometimes as high as one-
third of the inmate population.

The Juarez prison was quite an education for me. The officials
made a big deal about having two boys from the United States,
one white and one Indian. They decided, after fifty-five days, to
take us to Mexican court. We were marched back to the captain's
office to pick up our belongings. All we received were our empty
billfolds.

"Hey, man," I protested, "What about our rings and watches?"

"What rings? What watches? I don't remember you ever turning
in anything like that," he replied.

I began to see the handwriting on the wall. "Well, then, how
about our leather belts?" I asked.

"Sure thing," he agreed. "Just pick one off the rack."

Naturally, all that was left on the rack were belts that looked like
they'd been through the Civil War a time or two. Scotty and I
reached the same conclusion. "Naw, we'll pass."

Then six armed guards with 303 British Infield rifles marched
us out to a waiting car. There were three detectives in it. There was
a car in front of us with three armed guards, and a car behind us
with three armed guards. We made quite a procession as they took
us to the Mexican court. It was kind of a kangaroo court. The
magistrate simply told us that we were undesirable characters in

Mexico and we were to leave immediately. He put a three-year ban on us ever coming back in to his country again.

From there it was just a short walk across the bridge to our own country, but they really made a spectacle of it. The six armed guards marched three in front of us and three behind us. The detectives were on the side of us, while Scotty and I were handcuffed together. In this manner they marched us across the Rio Grande back onto U.S. soil.

When we reached the Customs inspection station on the United States side, we were turned over to the authorities there. The FBI was waiting for us. We traded our Mexican handcuffs for FBI handcuffs. Then we were taken down to the El Paso County Jail. It was really a relief to be back in our country. I turned to Scotty, "At least we're finally gonna get some food, man. No matter what it is, it's bound to be good compared to what we've been eating for the last two months."

In the federal marshal's office, federal charges were filed against Scotty and I for international transportation of stolen vehicles. Then we were put in a tank containing twenty-one "wetbacks"—Mexicans who had crossed the river to gain illegal entry into the U.S. We got there just in time for lunch. I couldn't believe my eyes. It was beans! They fed those wetback Mexicans on beans twice a day.

However, the next morning we did get coffee, rolls, and cereal. I would never have believed Post Toasties could taste so good.

CHAPTER 7

Getting Deeper
Into Trouble

While Scotty and I were in the county jail, we did some serious talking. "Scotty," I told him, "there's no reason for both of us to take a rap. I know I'm going to get some time because of my record, so I'll take the rap for this." Of course, he gratefully agreed.

There in the tank I met a Mexican-American who wanted to escape. He had some hacksaw blades that had been smuggled in to him in some comic books his family had slipped by the authorities. He asked me to help him in an escape attempt. Since I wanted out myself, I joined him.

We began to saw through the heavy ventilation bars that went into the main duct of the heating and air conditioning system of the jail and courthouse. We had to make a lot of different noises to cover up the sounds the hacksaw blades made on the heavy bars. Naturally the authorities in the jail heard those noises and constantly tried to track them down. We set little pieces of broken mirror out on the catwalk so we could spot any guard who tried to sneak up on us.

After several days, we had sawed a hole big enough for a man to crawl through. We were ready to go! But on the very day of our planned escape, the guards made a surprise shakedown. They discovered several pieces of our hacksaw blades. We had strung clothing on a line to screen the hole that we had cut. The guards jerked down the line and uncovered our escape route. There went the whole scheme. All that work down the drain. Well, we had always known the odds were considerably against us.

The officials emptied the tank and put us all in different cells. They gave us a pretty rough time for awhile. However, since we hadn't been caught in the act of escaping, they could not charge us with an attempted escape.

When Scotty and I went to court, the judge gave me four years federal time and Scotty four years probation. Thus ended our partnership and adventure. Scotty caught the bus back to Minneapolis, while I caught a marshal's car to the Federal Reformatory in El Reno, Oklahoma. Still, I wasn't too upset by the four-year sentence. I knew I could make parole in just a matter of eighteen months.

At El Reno I was marched through the gates, handcuffed and chained, and taken down to the main office for fingerprinting. My mug shot was taken again, after which a barber shaved my head. I don't know why this was done—perhaps to strip me of all humanity and make me feel as low a person as possible. Then that number, 33476SW, was attached to my clothes and I was sent over to A and O—Admissions and Orientation.

Several days later I had made a few friends and had finally gotten out into the main compound. There I found some of my old buddies from South Minneapolis. Tom was there, Dennis too, and several others I had known. It was like old home week.

I soon settled down and started pulling my time. I applied for vocational horticulture. This would mean a job out in the greenhouse which would put me outside the fences. There I would feel free for at least part of the day. I had been behaving myself quite well. The officials decided I'd be a good risk outside the fences. They reduced my security status from close to medium, so I was able to go with a guard outside the fences. A couple of months later my security was reduced to minimum. This meant that I was able to work out there on my own during the weekends, taking care of the greenhouse.

But I was still a con man. I had conned my way into that job to get outside the fences for a reason. There was a woman in Oklahoma City, a pharmaceutical assistant, who would steal Methedrine tablets and drop them at a certain spot beside the highway. I would pick them up, smuggle them into the institution, and sell them for a good price. I always had to have something going. Occasionally, I brought in some whiskey for my buddies and me. I was really trying to be cool.

During the time in El Reno, I met Bob, a smooth con man from Las Vegas, Nevada. Bob had been busted on an international charge of smuggling stolen furs into Canada and had landed in El Reno. He was also a jewel thief. We became good friends in the penitentiary. We knew we'd both be paroling about the same time, so we began to plan burglaries and heists. Most inmates talk about these things, but they never carry them off.

Sure enough, Bob and I were both released within a few months of each other. We jumped parole right away and started down the list. We pulled off nearly everything we'd planned there in prison—right down to the letter. In Oklahoma we busted a couple of thousand dollars worth of checks. We flew to New Orleans and scored. Then on we went to Miami, where we spent seven weeks burglarizing homes and pulling off con jobs.

There was a big diamond fence in Florida who told us he'd buy any diamonds we could get to him. So Bob and I planned a jewelry store heist. We had already bought a .25 caliber automatic pistol. I also carried a knife with me most of the time. We decided to pull a daylight armed robbery.

We had stolen a Buick Wildcat, a Hertz Rent-a-Car, and a Lincoln Continental. We would be switching cars three different times. We planned to dump two of them along the way after the robbery, so as not to leave much of a trail.

At the last minute I began to have second thoughts. "What if that guy in the jewelry store has a gun to defend himself? If it comes down to either me or him, I know I'd shoot him. Then I'd be facing a murder rap. That would be a life sentence or even the death penalty."

I expressed these doubts to Bob. "Man, what if something

goes wrong? I'm fed up with prison time. I don't want to go back again."

"Come on, Richard," Bob argued. "Nothing's gonna go wrong. How can we get caught? We've got this planned too smooth."

"No, I don't think so," I told him. "I don't really know why, but this is where I'm getting off." That day I packed my bags, took my stolen Wildcat, and left Daytona. Bob pulled off the jewelry store heist by himself. Sure enough he was busted and sent to Raiford State Penitentiary in Florida for ten years.

On my way from Daytona to Oklahoma City, I had a special way to finance the trip. My big thing was to stop at motels each night, sign the ticket, and then leave the next morning with their color TV set. Nearly every motel I stayed in had one less television when I left. Even though most motel sets have a sign on them, "Warning, this device is connected to a burglar alarm system in the manager's office," I knew it wasn't true. Ninety-nine out of a hundred of those signs are just stickers and a phony wire. So I'd rip them off and sell them in the next town at the pawn shop.

In Oklahoma City I decided I needed a new car. I traded off the Buick Wildcat for a hot, brand new 1969 Riviera. I scored again in Oklahoma City, and I picked up a twelve-gauge shotgun that I loaded and carried with me the rest of the way.

In Wichita, Kansas, I rented a little room at a motel called "The Pair-A-Dice Bar and Motel," a well-known hangout for hoodlums and criminal types. One day I went out to case some houses for planning burglaries. I would get the names and addresses off the mailboxes. Then I'd look up their phone numbers and call them to see when they would or wouldn't be home.

Intent on my search, I was startled when a motorcycle cop behind me motioned me to pull over. "Oh, no," I thought, "this is it." I pulled over and stopped, got out of the car, and stepped back to his motorcycle.

"May I see your license, sir?" he asked. I pulled it out of my wallet and handed it to him. "Are you aware that you were doing 55 in a 35 zone?"

"No, I didn't realize it," I replied politely. "I guess my mind was on other things. I just wasn't paying any attention."

"I have to write you a ticket, you know," he told me. "But first I have to check your car out."

"No problem," I lied. Convincingly, I hoped. "This is a company car. I'm a salesman for our Florida-based company." This lie was necessary since I had put stolen Florida plates on the car I had stolen in Oklahoma. The plates had come off a car which I'd noticed hadn't been driven in a long time at a large apartment complex close to my room.

The cop called in the plate numbers and sat there waiting for the reply over his radio. He had never gotten off his motorcycle. He removed his helmet and hung it on his handlebars. We waited silently. Tension stretched my nerves to the snapping point. Thoughts jumped through my mind, "What if the plates come back hot? He'll go for his gun and he'll call a squad car to come get me. I've got to get away!"

I waited, nerves knotted up. I got ready to jump him, to knock his motorcycle over on top of him and go for his gun as I did it. The radio crackled. "This is it, buddy," I told myself. "It's him or me. And I'm not going back to prison."

But the call came back through that the plates on my Riviera were clean. My knees almost wobbled with relief. The cop was saying, "Sorry for the inconvenience, sir, but it's my job to call in about out of state tags, you understand."

"Sure. Like I said, no problem."

He cranked his bike and pulled away, never knowing how close he had come to being the victim of an all-out attack.

Three days later I was out in front of my motel washing the Riviera. Suddenly a car pulled up in front of the motel. I smelled "cop" right away and headed for my room. My shotgun was loaded, leaning up against the wall right behind the door. A voice yelled, "Halt"' I stopped and slowly turned around. He had his gun pointed at me.

Two men put me up against the brick wall of the motel and

frisked me. "He's clean," one commented. They turned me around, handcuffed me, put me in a squad car, and headed downtown.

"Hey, what's all this about?" I protested.

"You'll find out later. Meanwhile, you have the right to . . ."

"Yeah, yeah, yeah, I know."

Later, I discovered that the motorcycle cop who pulled me over had come across a hot sheet on me. He turned it in to the FBI, and they came to get me.

Charges of parole violation were filed against me. The sheriff's deputy took me up the Sedgwick County Jail. Inside I found two of my old buddies—one from El Reno and another from a jail several years back. It never failed. Wherever I went to jail, I always had friends.

In about a month, the federal marshals picked me up and took me back to El Reno. New federal charges were filed on me—two counts of the Dyer Act (one on the Buick Wildcat from Miami Beach to Oklahoma City, and on the Buick Riviera from Oklahoma City to Wichita, Kansas). The federal judge in Oklahoma City handed down two three-year consecutive sentences on top of the balance of my present four-year sentence. I immediately applied for a sentence reduction, hoping to get my consecutive sentences changed into concurrent sentences—in other words, to have them run together. But the judge wouldn't do it. He did give me an A2 number before each sentence. This entitled me to make parole immediately on each sentence, so I wouldn't have to pull a certain amount of time on each one of them. In the long run this did help.

For now, I was back where I hated to be—behind bars. I had managed to stay out of El Reno only seven weeks.

CHAPTER 8

Freedom Behind Bars

El Reno was a tough prison. In my three and a half years there, there wasn't much I did not see or hear. I saw several inmates die from beatings and stabbings. There was always something going on—homosexualism, dope, illegal card games, gambling. Never a dull moment.

The homosexual ratio at El Reno is very high. There was so much of it, I finally got used to seeing it. It became so commonplace to me that I didn't even look twice. I just went about my business.

It wasn't long before I got into drugs again. One day a fellow crossed me on a drug deal. He didn't pay off what he had bought, so I threatened him with his life. "Three days, pal; that's all you've got," I warned. "You either come across with the money or you're a dead man." That same evening he checked himself into Cellhouse B for protection. He not only had me on his back, but several other inmates he had burned were out to get him as well. We put so much pressure on him that he felt there was only one way out. That night in Cellhouse B he slashed his wrists. The guards found him in time, though. He didn't die.

Fortunately, none of this came to the surface. My name was never mentioned. As far as the authorities were concerned, I was a pretty good inmate. I was always very discreet in everything I did, never letting on that I was into anything illegal. By seeming to mind my own business, by saying "Yes sir and No sir" to the guards, I put on a pretty good con job.

The fellow who had the next bunk to me was named Rule. He had three days to go before he made parole. He was really excited about it, making all kinds of plans. That afternoon during four o'clock count, Rule didn't show up to his bunk. We were counted again, and was still missing. He was off work. There was no reason for him to be out of the dorm to miss count. Out went the alarm.

Whenever someone was missing, all the inmates in the institution were kept locked up while the guards searched the grounds for him. They hunted Rule about half an hour. I was standing on a bunk looking out the window when a guard yelled, "I found him." He'd found Rule all right—hanging by his own belt. Broken nose, broken jaw, busted up ribs. It seems there had been several men who wanted to use Rule for their homosexual urges, but he wouldn't submit. So he had been nearly beaten to death and then hung. Three days short of parole.

Timothy was another friend of mine. He worked in the carpenter shop, so whenever he could get it he sniffed glue to get high. One day a guard caught him at it and busted him. He started taking Timothy over to Cellhouse B. Timothy did not want to go, so he broke loose. He ran through the yard as fast as he could. Right in front of Guntower One he attempted to go over the fence. The guard aimed his shotgun out the window, yelling for Timothy to stop. But Timothy was desperate. He kept climbing up and up and up—whether to freedom or to suicide. As Timothy topped the fence under the guard tower, the guard pulled the trigger. Timothy fell dead on the freedom side of the fence.

For about a year I lived in Unit Five. We had individual cells there. One Saturday morning as I lay in my bunk reading, I heard a noise out in the hallway. Curious, I put down my book, opened my door, and stepped out. A Spanish boy down on all fours was crawling toward me. Blood continuously dripped on the floor each time he moved. As I shouted for the guard, the boy fell to the floor, unconscious. That morning as he laid resting with his blanket pulled up over his head, two inmates had sneaked in on him. One hit him over the head with a pipe, and the other stabbed him a dozen times. All this over a bad dope deal. The hospital orderlies brought over a stretcher and carted him off. Fortunately, the boy lived. And thus began another "peaceful weekend" at El Reno. It didn't really even faze me. I had seen so many things like this before, I figured there wasn't anything anywhere that could shake me.

Most of the inmates in prison take advantage of the sports activities offered them if for no other reason than to work out their aggressions and get bone tired. After a hard game of tennis or handball or after lifting heavy weights, we'd fall asleep instead of lying awake thinking about home and families and freedom.

I hit the weight pile. It seemed like all the heavies on the compound were weight lifters. They had their own little clique—a rugged group. The first time I ever did a bench press it was 155 pounds. I worked out every day. A year and a half later I was lifting 285 pounds. Mainly I wanted to build my strength. I felt I always had to come out on top in a fight or whatever was going on. Many times I used my size just to bluff a person. I had developed a big mouth as well, to use on people I didn't like, to more or less scare them into doing what I wanted. I quickly put people wise to the fact that they were not to tangle with me unless they wanted to wind up in bad shape.

One "wise old saying" in the penitentiary goes like this: "If we can't get along, let's get it on." That became my personal motto. I would fight anybody, anytime, any place—it made no difference to me. The great confidence I had in myself always seemed to work to my advantage.

Always, always I longed for freedom. I had been back in prison about six months when I learned what REAL freedom meant. The date was Sunday, March 16, 1969. It started out no different from any other Sunday. I got up early that morning and went over to the chow hall for breakfast. Sitting there over a bowl of cereal and a cup of coffee, I noticed quite a few free world men standing around chatting with some of the inmates. I wondered what was going on. Then my eyes caught on a big sign that announced:

Christian Business Men's Committee
Meeting with Inmates in the Chapel
Rap Sessions—Bible Studies—Testimonies
Singing—Preaching
All Day Fellowship! EVERYONE WELCOME!

"Fellowship?" "Testimonies?" I didn't know what any of it meant. "Well, I just might mosey on over there to see what's happening," I decided. Anything new would serve to break the monotony of prison life.

After breakfast, I wandered over to the chapel just to see if anything interesting was developing. The program was just beginning. A man about sixty-five years old met me at the door, shook my hand, and introduced himself as Mr. Hilton from Enid, Oklahoma. I told him my name and asked what was going on.

"Well, we are just a group of Christian businessmen from different denominations who have come out here to put on a program for the inmates," he replied. "I wish you'd stay and listen awhile, Richard."

"Sure. Why not?" I agreed, picking out a place to sit. I didn't realize what was coming.

There were probably about forty free world men there and about fifty inmates who stayed to listen to the program. They sang a few songs before the preacher got up to speak. His words just went in one of my ears and out the other. My mind drifted back to the time I was in the Hennepin County Jail. Back then the Salvation Army people would come in every Sunday to sing to us, attempt to tell their testimonies and preach. Invariably, every Sunday some of the inmates would throw dirty toilet water on those people or spit at them, curse them, and run them out. Still they came back to try again and again.

"And here are some others," I thought as the man preached that day. I didn't really pay attention to his sermon at all. I was more interested in these people who had come. I realized how vastly different their lives were from mine.

This was only the second time in my life I'd been to church. Both times were in the prison chapel. The first time I was in orientation and required to go. This time I had come out of curiosity. "I've never been to Sunday School in my life," I recalled, "nor read the Bible. I've never even really prayed in my whole life. Sure, I believe there's probably a God somewhere," I acknowledged to myself, "but even so, He's no doubt given up on me a long time ago." I certainly did not know anything about God. I was totally ignorant of anything spiritual.

My attention came back into focus. The preacher had sat down. The men sang a couple of songs I didn't know. Then a man from Kansas City, Kansas stood up. He was redheaded like me. Mr. Hutchenson was his name. "Fellows, I've sat where you're now sitting," he told us. "I served seven years in the state penitentiary at Lansing, Kansas. But while I was there, something fantastic happened. You know what it was?" All eyes were on him. We were silent, alert, waiting. He continued, "It was this: One day a man came to tell me that Jesus Christ would save me and forgive me of my sins and change my life if I'd let Him. I hated the way my life was going. I decided, Why not give this Jesus a chance?" He went on to share how he gave his life to Christ and was truly a changed man. He was finally paroled from prison and now he is a businessman in Kansas City. Mr. Hutchenson assured us that he is still serving the Lord Jesus Christ, first of all.

When Mr. Hutchenson sat down, a black fellow named Benjamin Franklin stood up. He smiled a beautiful smile and said, "I, too, once longed for freedom as you do now. I spent fifteen years in Lansing State Penitentiary. Yes, I knew Mr. Hutchenson there. In fact, I was the fellow who led him to the Lord, after I had found Jesus as my Savior in a service similar to this one today." He paused a moment, seeming to measure his words carefully. Then he earnestly told us, "I had searched every avenue of life for meaning and purpose and happiness. It was not to be found until I invited Jesus Christ into my heart. That day I asked Him to forgive me of my sins, Jesus set me free from Satan's power and changed my life completely." Again that beautiful smile. "I, too, am now a businessman out in the free world serving Jesus Christ."

Questions pounded through my head. "Set free? How can this be? Who is this Jesus Christ? The man I've seen in pictures hanging on a cross? If he's dead, how can he change anything?"

It was time for the rap session. Even though I wanted to know more, I wouldn't express the thoughts buzzing through my mind. I had a lot of pride. I didn't want the other inmates to think I was interested in any kind of religion bit. But I listened. How I listened—intently! There seemed to be something deep inside me beginning to stir.

Mr. Hilton had remained by my side. It was about two o'clock. We were sitting in a back pew of the El Reno Chapel. He turned to me and very kindly asked, "Richard, are you a Christian? Are you saved?"

Well, I really didn't know what "a Christian" was. I didn't know what "saved" meant either. But I knew I was neither. "No sir," I replied, "I don't think so."

"Have you ever read the Bible, Richard?"

"No, never," I admitted.

Mr. Hilton persisted, "Do you know anything at all about Jesus?"

"No, not really. I've never been to church. I know Jesus was a good man, and I've seen pictures of Him hanging on a cross."

"Yes, this is why, Richard." Mr. Hilton opened the big Bible he was carrying. "Look at this verse. It is John 3:16." Then he read it to me. "For God so loved the world that he gave His only begotten Son that whosoever believeth in Him should not perish but have everlasting life."

Here I was twenty-four years old, and this was the first time I'd ever heard of John 3:16. The words sank in. "Loved." "Gave." "Only Son."

"But, Richard," Mr. Hilton continued, "Jesus didn't stay dead! He rose from the grave on the third day. That is why we celebrate Easter today—to celebrate Jesus' coming out of that tomb and bringing life to all of us! New life. Life that had never been given before. Everlasting life."

Next my friend turned to Romans 3:23 and read it to me. "For all have sinned and come short of the glory of God." Then to Romans 6:23, "For the wages of sin is death, but the gift of God is eternal life through Jesus Christ our Lord." God's Word was coming on strong! Then Mr. Hilton put Romans 10:9 in front of me. "If thou shalt confess with thy mouth the Lord Jesus, and shalt believe in thine heart that God hath raised Him from the dead, thou shalt be saved," I read.

"Now drop down to verse thirteen," he instructed.

"For whosoever shall call upon the name of the Lord shall be saved." Whosoever—that meant anyone, didn't? Even me.

"Richard," Mr. Hilton asked carefully, "do you want to be saved, be changed today?"

Man, what a heavy question! "W-e-l-l," I began.

"Let me put it this way," he said. "Richard, think about this: Where have you come from? Where are you going?"

For the first time in my life I took a long, hard look at my past. All I saw was hatred and bitterness and heartache and sorrow. Jail cell after jail cell after jail cell. That's where I'd come from. Where was I going? When I looked into the future, all I saw was more bitterness, more hatred, more sorrow, and many more jail cells. Suddenly the sight was unbearable to me.

I heard Mr. Hilton saying, "Richard, Jesus Christ can save you and change your life if you'll repent of your sins. Are you ready to turn from your evil ways, to have a new life?"

"Yes sir, I am."

"Well, kneel right here with me and let's pray." He began to get on his knees.

I looked up to find several of my inmate buddies watching me. All my pride rose up fast. In the penitentiary only sissies get on their knees. I paused. "Can't we pray just sitting here on the pew?" I asked.

He looked at me a long moment. Then he said, "Yes, we can. It doesn't really matter WHERE you repent, so long as you do. but I wish you'd kneel down here with me."

At that very moment the Holy Spirit penetrated my hard shell of bitterness and melted my pride. I got down on my knees, not caring what anybody else thought. Mr. Hilton placed his hand on my shoulder and simply said, "God, hear this young man's prayer. Save his soul, change his life. Thank you, Lord Jesus. Amen!" Then he said, "Now it's your turn, Richard. Won't you ask Jesus to come into your life?"

I knew I was a sinner and that if I remained like I was, I'd die in my sins and go to hell. I realized that Jesus Christ had died for me. God gave his only son for ME. He loved me that much. The only way I knew how, I prayed. "Lord Jesus, if you are who you say you are, if you can do what this man says you can do and what the Bible says you can do in my life, please come do it. Forgive me of my sins. Make me the kind of person You want me to be. Thank you. Amen."

Instantly I knew that *this was what I'd been looking for all my life.* I felt different. I knew that Jesus had really saved me, because I felt clean inside. A few seconds before, I had been blind, but now I could see that God's Word was inspired Truth. Most of all, I was finally free! Really free. Free from sin, free from hatred and bitterness, free from my past. I was a new man. I had been set free—born again. Praise the Living God!

I realized that these Christian men who came to the penitentiary that day were real men, led by the Holy Spirit. Prior to this, I had thought a man was somebody tough who could out-fight, out-drink, out-cuss, and out-smoke everybody else. I discovered that a real man was someone who could stand up for Jesus. A real man could share Jesus with somebody who needed Him. A real man was someone who followed Jesus all the way.

Mr. Hilton gave me a New Testament with his name and address in it so I could write to him. He took down my name and number. He shared some parting thoughts, shook my hand, and said goodbye. I went back to my cell. But I went back as a changed man, a different person—all because one man had taken the time to come share Jesus Christ with me.

Because of one man who cared,
He went to prison and shared.

He shared of Christ's death at dear Calvary,
And how He died for you and me.

There in the cell a prisoner had prayer
And accepted Christ because one man did care.
Then that prisoner cared by preaching God's Word,
How God can save men by trusting the Lord.

He showed me the Bible and told me to pray.
I was so happy for I received Christ that day.
Thank God for that man who came to prison with love,
For now I am going to Heaven above!

(by Lenita Levan,
who was led to Jesus Christ
by Richard Coss)

The Bill Glass Prison Crusade Team before entering the Oklahoma State Penitentiary for three days of soul-winning. The author did the "death row" follow-up for five weeks.

CHAPTER 9

New Meaning to Life

From that day on, I had a different attitude and outlook on life. For the first time, my life had meaning and purpose. After I had been saved only a couple of hours, Jesus Christ—through the power of the Holy Spirit—began to work a new purpose in my heart. I suddenly realized a love for my fellow inmates. Not a homosexual love or a worldly love. No, this was a God-given love for their souls.

I had finally found the life I always longed for, and I knew it was *the only life* for me—living in Jesus Christ. Jesus gave me a reason for going straight, for obeying the law. One by one I gave all my problems to Him. My filthy, cursing mouth was cleansed by the blood of Jesus. My ferocious, violent temper was controlled by the power of the Holy Spirit. Christ took away my desire for alcohol and drugs. But He never left me hanging, groping in thin air, or grasping for something to fill the void. Every time He took away an old, filthy habit, He replaced it with a new desire. I now longed to be like Jesus, to be one of His own, showing love, joy, peace, patience, kindness, and other virtues—which are the products of the Holy Spirit.

As I changed inside, I even began to change physically. I gained weight because my burdens were lifted. I no longer lay awake on my cot worrying. Each night I trusted the Lord to give me a good night's rest, and He always did. Yes, I had this assurance from

God because He said it in His Word. I had started reading the Bible and claiming every promise in there as my very own.

I wanted to know more about the Christ who saved me. I realized I had been saved to serve my Lord right there in the penitentiary. He had given me a job to do. I went to see Chaplain Diamond and told him what had happened to me. He was a born-again man, so he understood and rejoiced with me.

"Richard," he said, "you really need to get into God's Word. A real knowledge and understanding of His Word will take you through the hard times ahead. Why don't you take a Bible course?"

"Sure, I'd like to. But how can I?"

"Well, there are several good correspondence courses offered," he assured me, pulling out a list from his desk.

So I took all the courses the institution offered—from the Assemblies of God, the Salvation Army, the Prison Mission Association, the Berean Bible Studies. The denomination didn't matter to me. I took them all. They were laying the bedrock of truth in a heart that had only had shifting sands. I studied three hours a day and memorized the Word of God as I worked on those Bible study courses. How I longed to know more about God! My past had been filled with pornography and garbage. Now I wanted to read the living Word of God. In eighteen months I had completed all the study courses.

Then, I also began to read the books Christian people brought to me, such as *Run, Baby Run, The Cross and the Switchblade, Twelve Angels from Hell, Peril By Choice, Through Gates of Splendor,* and many more. As I read missionary stories and exciting accounts of Christ-changed lives, I knew He had truly changed my life as much as anyone I read about. It was thrilling!

The guards noticed a change in me. The other inmates noticed it too, especially when I began to share Christ with them. I had realized that I, too, could tell people about Jesus. The power of the Holy Spirit could help me win people to Christ. I thought everybody ought to know what I had found.

For several weeks my inmate buddies watched me. One later confessed, "Richard, we knew you were a con man. You were up for parole before too long, so we figured you'd lay a big snow job on the parole judge with a 'What a good Christian I am' routine." I knew what they thought. I knew a great many of them looked at me with scorn and contempt. But, I didn't care. My new life was worth it. I went right on studying my Bible and doing my correspondence courses. Every time the chapel door was open, I headed over there, carrying my Bible and usually taking at least one inmate with me. After several months, my inmate friends realized that my experience was going to stick. It was real. One by one they dropped by my cell. "Rich," they all advised, "if this is going to keep you straight, you hang in there. Don't ever let anybody take it away from you."

I would always tell them, "Man, I'm going to. But, how about you?"

The reactions to this question varied. Sometimes my friends said, "Oh, that's not my bag right now. I want to live a bit yet. When I get old, I might turn on to Jesus." Another would hang his head and mumble, "I'll think about it, Rich." Still I kept on telling them about how Jesus loved them.

Finally, came the day I'll never forget. Two of my friends asked, "How can we be saved, Rich? How do we get this peace and joy and freedom you're always talking about?" When this happened, I realized I didn't even know how to pray for them or lead them in prayer. So I turned to the sinner's prayer I had written down and taped into my Bible and said, "I want you to read this prayer, and believe in your hearts, and God will save you. That's all." And so they did—and God did! Right then I found out there were two great joys in life: receiving Christ in your own heart and then leading others to Him. Both of these men are still serving God, working in their local churches. One is in Chicago, and the other in Baton Rouge, Louisiana. Christ changed their lives, just as He had changed mine.

The rest of my time in prison began to fly by. I worked hard. I spent every spare moment of my time in God's Word, reading and studying. Whatever God had planned for me in the future, it was going to be good, and I was determined to be well prepared.

The parole judge came and went, leaving me with a little more time to serve yet. Still I was learning. Every Tuesday night the Christian Businessmen would come in and share more about Christ with us. I thank God for that group of dedicated men. They not only taught us more of Jesus, they also warned us against Satan, who goes about as a roaring lion to destroy anyone he can (I Peter 5:8). They instructed us how to put on the whole armor of God in order to be protected from the assaults of the devil (Ephesians 6:11, 17).

For fourteen years I had served Satan. I'd smoked, drank, and fought in public. I had committed crimes out where everybody could see me—never ashamed of anything I did. Now I was bound and determined to live for Christ just as boldly. I would talk about Jesus in public. I would live for Him in public. And I would *never be ashamed* of Him (Mark 8:38). "For God has not given us the spirit of fear, but of power and of love and of a sound mind. Be not thou therefore ashamed of the testimony of our Lord, nor of me his prisoner" (II Timothy 1:7-8).

The warden at El Reno was a Christian also, and he understood the drastic difference in me. In fact, he let me go on Sundays to preach and give my testimony in churches around El Reno, or to speak to prayer groups or Christian Businessmen's conventions. Man, it was an exciting way of doing time!

Finally, I made parole. When I met my parole officer, I discovered he was a born-again Christian, too. We hardly even discussed my parole situation. We talked about soul-winning and lives being changed. Thank God for Christian parole officers who understand. Today, my former parole officer is one of my best friends. I've gotten to know his whole family.

CHAPTER 10

Freedom

On November 12, 1970, at 8:05 a.m. I walked out of the prison gates for the last time. I knew I would never be back behind bars, except to witness to others about Jesus. Now I was free both inside and out. Whoever Jesus sets free is free indeed! (John 8:36)

Claude Ohnsman, a good Christian friend and brother who had been influential in my salvation, met me at the gate. We drove straight to the little Baptist Church where I'd been baptized. There we knelt to pray and begin my new life in the free world the right way. Claude and many other Christian friends gave of their time and money to help me get established. One helped me find an apartment. Another sold me a car. Since Claude was a painting contractor, he painted my apartment. People brought over pots and pans, dishes, rugs, even a television set, and gave them all to me.

"Why are you people doing this?" I kept asking, hardly able to take it all in. "Why do this for me?"

"Richard, we love you in Christ," they told me. "We want to help you get on your feet so you will be able to help other people someday." It was fantastic. It was beautiful. It was God's love being poured out to me through His People.

I determined right then that, with God's help, I *would* someday be in a position to help others as I had been helped. In Ephesians 4:28, God's Word says, "Let the thief no longer steal, but rather let him labor doing honest work with his hands that he may be able to give to those in need." I was now living in Christ. I had become a new creature. Old things had passed away. Everything had become new (II Corinthians 5:17). It was a new life—an exciting way to walk.

Now that I was out on the streets I wanted to witness even more. God just kept my time occupied. He gave me a good job. he saw to it I was called upon many, many times to give my testimony in different meetings and churches. I still can't think of anything better to do than to testify for my Lord Jesus. Everywhere I went I told people about Christ and my personal experience with Him. I always asked them, "Has this ever happened to you?"

My new life was thrilling, just being led by the Holy Spirit day by day, hour by hour, minute by minute. Never knowing nor caring what was around the next corner, simply trusting that "all things work together for good to them that love God, to them who are called according to His purpose" (Romans 8:28). That was my life's motto. Sure, I had problems now and then. But, Jesus Christ was and is always the problem solver. He told me in His Word to cast all my burdens, my cares, my worries on Him, and He would carry the load for me (Matthew 11:28). I not only believed them, I proved it in my own life as I stood on the promises of the Word of God.

As I settled into my little apartment, I found that God was continuing to put many fine, soul-winning Christians in my path so I could continue to grow in fellowship.

I soon received a call from First Southern Baptist Church of Del City, Oklahoma, asking me to share my testimony in a Sunday morning service. Dr. Jimmy Draper met me that morning and accompanied me to the platform, introducing me as the guest speaker. There were about 2,000 people looking at me as I shared how Jesus Christ changed my life.

As my eyes glanced over the crowd I noticed something you don't see in most churches today: blacks were seated next to whites and the poor were seated next to the rich. A young man around 18 years old with long hair pulled back into a ponytail and wearing a muscle shirt sat next to a man wearing a very expensive suit, and they were all loving me. Needless to say, I joined that church the following Sunday. I had been praying for God to lead me to a loving, soul-winning church, and He did.

Seven months later, in June 1971, I married a young lady who I had met at a Bible study. We were married for fifteen years. Shortly after our marriage Dr. Draper preached my ordination service, and the church put their stamp of approval on my life and ministry to preach the Good News of Jesus Christ.

A year later a little redheaded baby girl was born to us and we named her Edye Ann. Seven years later we adopted an eleven-year-old boy named Danny. Our family was growing and so was the ministry God had given to us.

Richard and Phyllis Coss, 1988.

CHAPTER 11

Following and Fishing

"Follow me, and I will make you fishers of men." Jesus promised in Matthew 4:19. If you follow Jesus, you will always be fishing for men's souls. If you're not fishing, you're not following closely enough. My fishing holes are often bars, nightclubs, and dope dens—anywhere I see people crying out against the darkness of their lives. They don't even realize themselves that their actions clearly picture the agonizing cries of their hearts: "Oh, I'm miserable. I'm lonely. I'm frustrated. I'm lost. Won't somebody please come tell me about Jesus?" Then, they try one thing after another to shut off that cry. Booze. Sex. Excitement. Tranquilizers. But, nothing really works. So they wait day after day for someone to shine light into their darkness—to tell them about the greatest thing that has ever happened to us: being saved. Accepting Jesus. Having our lives changed. Becoming a new creation!

Meeting Jesus is the greatest experience that can ever happen to anyone. He alone turns night into day, sorrow into laughter, broken homes into loving families. Before lost people need to know *anything* else, they need to discover the risen, living Savior who wants to dwell in their hearts—Jesus Christ.

As I said earlier, I realized on March 16, 1969, when God saved me, that I was saved to serve. Since that time I have continued to believe it and act like it. Sure, sometimes I get tired or discouraged. But in times like that a still voice within reminds me, "What if Mr. Hilton had been too tired to drive the sixty miles from Enid, Oklahoma to the El Reno prison to tell you about Jesus. Where would you be today?" I say, "Thank you, Lord, that he obeyed the Holy Spirit's call in his life that day to go visit a prisoner in prison."

Jesus said, in Matthew 25a:35-36, "I was thirsty, and you gave me drink. . . . I was sick and you visited me: I was in prison, and you came unto me." When the people ask, "Lord, when did we do all this for you?" Jesus will reply, "Inasmuch as you have done it unto one of the least of these my brethren, you have done it unto me." (Matthew 25:40)

So I realized today that I have a job to do—not because I have to, but because I *want* to share Christ with the people I meet every day. I want to follow Jesus and be a fisher of men. That's the reason I keep my fishing tackle in good shape. And I've had some interesting "fish" to take the best bait they had ever come across. I'd like to share some of these "fish stories" with you. There were some, you will see, who ignored me and others who cursed me. But many, many have been brought into the net of safety, that is, Jesus Christ. You can be sure of one thing, unlike most fish stories, these accounts are all true.

The Lonely Divorcee

One afternoon I went to the home of a young lady named Bobbie. Only twenty-four years old, she had already been married three times. Bobbie had two children, neither from any of the previous marriages. They were both illegitimate.

As I sat there with her, Bobbie began to unload. She talked and talked, detailing her loneliness and misery and frustration. She had been used and discarded by one man after another, leaving her hurt, bitter, broken. "Oh, I don't know why my life's in such a mess," she despaired.

"It doesn't have to be that way, Bobbie," I gently reassured her.

"Jesus can make a new life for you, a new person out of you." I told her about real love, true love, lasting love—God's love for her.

Tears welled up in her eyes and spilled down her cheeks as she decided, "I want this new life you're talking about. I want this person of Christ in my heart and life." Right there we knelt together as Bobbie invited Jesus to take charge of the shambles of her life. "Help me, Jesus," she wept. "Please give me a fresh start in life."

Jesus heard her pitiful cry. He came to fill her heart with His love. Almost immediately her countenance began to change. She looked softer, sweeter, and so much happier. Today Bobbie has been baptized. She joined a good church and she works for Jesus every day.

The Station Attendant

One night about eleven o'clock I pulled into a service station to get some gas. As the station attendant was filling my tank, we struck up a conversation. His name was Bob, and he hadn't been working there long.

"Right off the top of my head, I'd say we have something in common," he joked. We laughed, realizing what he meant. The bright lights highlighted our red hair.

Then we got down to serious business about Jesus. I gave Bob my testimony, and shared the Roman Road to salvation with him. Bob listened. He bowed his head and said yes to Jesus Christ, right there at the gas pump.

The next day I stopped in to see him. I was informed that just a couple of hours earlier the FBI had arrested Bob and taken him back to Texas. Bob had to go to prison, but he went as a missionary for Jesus Christ. God's timing is always perfect. The day before had been Bob's divine appointment, so that he might not go to prison lost, but safe in Jesus.

The Panhandler

One day I was standing on a street corner in Eugene, Oregon passing out tracts to those who walked by. Shuffling up the sidewalk came a great big fellow, a panhandler. He was about six foot six, had a pack on his back, a floppy old leather hat on his head, and a big bushy beard. He obviously hadn't taken a bath or cleaned up for quite a while. He wasn't too neat with the lump of tobacco he chewed. It was not only wadded up in his beard, it dripped onto his T-shirt leaving dark, smelly stains.

As the man walked by, I held out a tract. "Friend," I said, "here's something for you to read. God loves you and I love you."

He stopped right there in front of me, slowly turned, and stared down at me. Suddenly a stream of tobacco juice was coming at me. I jumped out of the way, and it hit the sidewalk.

"You still love?" he challenged.

I drew in a deep breath and hung onto my temper. "Yes," I told him. "But more important than that, God loves you."

"Well," he drawled, "if you love me so much—kiss me!"

Then he reached down and grabbed me. His lips were all puckered up. I turned my head away just in time. He plastered a big, juicy kiss on my cheek, leaving a wad of tobacco on the side of my face. He thought it was terribly funny. Somehow, I didn't.

I looked him straight in the eye, shook my head, and wiped off my cheek. "Friend, if you think this is love, you're really missing the boat. Real love is knowing Jesus as your personal Saviour. It was true love that sent Christ to die on a cross for you."

"Oh, shut up," he commanded. "I don't want to hear any of that garbage about God." He emphasized his point with a string of curse words and stomped away.

About ten minutes later, as I was strolling up the sidewalk, I saw him duck into a doorway trying to roll a cigarette. He saw me coming and braced himself. "Friend, I've still got something to say to you," I told him.

"No, you don't, you fanatic. Get away from me. I don't want to hear nothing you've got to say."

"Listen, you," I said, pointing my finger at him, "God sent me two thousand miles to tell you about His Son, Jesus, and I'm going to."

"I don't care if God dropped you out of the sky," he sneered. "Either you get away from me or we're going to fight."

"Man, I don't want to fight you—I want to help you," I said earnestly. "You need Jesus in your heart and life. Don't you realize he *died* for you?" Again he got mad and stomped off.

About an hour later, a group of us Christians were congregating in the shopping mall. A couple of teenagers were playing guitars, and we were all singing and praising God while we passed out tracts. Here came the big old panhandler. Since he had given me a little trouble earlier, I kept my eye on him now. He didn't even glance our way, but he shuffled by very slowly. I could tell he was listening to the message the kids were singing. In his hand he held a tract one of them had shared with him.

Later we prayed especially that God would touch this man's heart through the power of the Holy Spirit. It sure looked like God was working in his life. We committed him to the Lord's care, for we had done all we could. What an experience that was! Let me tell you, witnessing for Jesus Christ is never dull.

The Young Prostitute

One very cold winter morning I pulled into downtown Minneapolis at 4:00 A.M. As I stopped for a red light, I noticed a young girl on the other side of the intersection. She had her thumb out, begging for a ride. It was nine degrees below zero. I knew she must be freezing.

The light changed and I pulled over to pick her up. As she climbed in, the smell of booze emanating from her nearly knocked me over. "Been to a party?" I guessed.

"Yeah, but it was a bummer, so I'm going back to my own pad."

"My name's Richard," I told her. "What's yours?"

"Kay," she replied disinterestedly.

"Do you go to school or work or what?"

She looked straight at me and defiantly said, "I turn tricks for a living." Now, that did not mean she was part of an acrobatic act. Kay had just said she was a prostitute. She then asked, "You from around here?"

"I grew up here, but now live in Oklahoma. I'm just up for a visit with my mom."

"Did you bring any drugs with you?" she inquired.

"No, I didn't bring any drugs, but I brought something better than any drug ever could be."

"Really?" She perked up, interested now. "What's that?"

"His name is Jesus. He is God's Son, and you might think of Him as a 'supernatural high' because He'll never let you down." She sat silent, stunned. So I gently asked, "Kay, are you really happy living like you do?"

Great big tears welled up in her eyes, spilled over, and ran down her cheeks. "No, I haven't been really happy for a long, long time. To tell you the truth, it's been so long I can't even remember what being happy feels like."

For the next half hour as we sat in the warm car with icy winds howling outside, Kay told me her story—jail, reform school, then prostitution. Now only 20 years old, Kay had been selling her body to buy drugs and pay the rent for three and a half years.

When she finished, I began to tell Kay *my* story—jail, reform school, stealing to buy booze and drugs and to pay the rent. Her eyes grew wider and wider as she listened, for she realized that my past life was much like her present life. Finally, she broke in breathlessly, "But, you are not like that now! You're different. Tell me, *how did you change?* I've tried a million times to turn over a new leaf, but in a week's time I'm right back in the same rut."

So I told Kay about the Christian man who came to prison to tell me about Jesus Christ, about how I accepted Jesus as my Saviour and let *Him* change me. I explained how she, too, could be changed so that it would last. "Look at this, Kay," I said, showing her I Corinthians 6:9, 10, and 11 in *The Living Bible.* "Don't you know that those doing such things have no share in the Kingdom of God? Don't fool yourselves. Those who live immoral lives, who are idol worshippers, adulterers or homosexuals will have no share in His kingdom. Neither will thieves or greedy people, drunkards, slanderers, or robbers."

We were silent a moment, while what we had just read sank into her heart. "Kay, do you want Jesus to wash your sins away and change your life so you will be accepted by God?" I asked at last.

"Yes," she said simply, "I do."

We clasped hands and bowed our heads. Kay confessed her sins and unbelief to God, haltingly and hesitantly at first. But as the Holy Spirit truly broke through her shell of bitterness, she cried, "Oh Jesus, save me! Come into my life! Clean me up, make me what you want me to be." At last she raised her head. "He's doing it," she sobbed. "Jesus is washing out my life. I feel clean—really clean!" As we rejoiced together, there was a little bit of heaven in that car.

Before I left the city, I took Kay to meet many new brothers and sisters in Jesus. They began working with Kay, helping her to become a real disciple.

The Lost Daughter

In Verden, Oklahoma, I was preaching a revival at the United Methodist Church. One evening a couple came forward during the invitation. They were friends I hadn't seen in about two years. The wife was crying as they knelt at the altar. As I asked her what was wrong, I saw a shudder shake her shoulders. She told me her daughter Shelly had been arrested on drug charges the day before and was at that moment sitting in the county jail in Chickasha. She asked me to go visit Shelly, and I promised I would.

After the meeting ended, I went across the street to the house where I was staying. The Lord spoke to me, telling me to go to the jail right then. I wasn't to wait until the next day. For a second I wondered how on earth I'd get into a county jail at 11:30 at night, but then I realized there is nothing impossible with God's help. Since He had told me to go, I knew the Holy Spirit would go ahead of me to open the jail doors. Jerry Scott, the singer in my meeting, went with me.

Sure enough, the Lord had gone before us. When we approached the officer on duty that evening, told him who we were and what we wanted, he told us to go right on up.

Upstairs in the women's tank, there on the bunk sat one lonely, frustrated, scared eighteen-year-old. "Hi, Shelly," I said.

She looked up. "Who are you?"

"My name is Richard. I'm a friend of your folks." I began to share Jesus Christ with Shelly. When I asked if she wanted to be saved that evening, she broke down and began to cry. "Oh, I'm scared. I just want out of here!"

"Shelly," I told her, "if you leave this place without Jesus, chances are you'll soon be back in again. But the Bible says that Jesus came to set the captive free. He will set you really free tonight, if you only let Him."

Suddenly she screamed, "I can't, I can't, I can't accept Christ!"

Sin had a hard grip on that young lady's life. I recognized that she was being tormented by Satan. "Shelly, grab my hand," I directed, reaching through the bars. As she clutched my hand, I began to pray in the name of Jesus, commanding Satan to leave that jail cell, to loose his hold on Shelly. We prayed for quite some time. Then I gave her a New Testament to read. Before we left, Jerry walked up to the bars and sang a gospel song to Shelly, while I knelt praying in the hallway. I knew there were other prisoners on the men's side listening. A couple of policemen downstairs were listening. Momentarily I thought, "Isn't this something? Praying and singing hymns at midnight in the jailhouse. This is how Paul and Silas felt, praising God even though they were on the other side of the bars."

The next day Shelly's mom and dad made her bail. That night they came to the revival. God anointed me as I preached. At the invitation, many decisions for Christ were made. But Shelly didn't come.

I knew God was stirring her. I knew that deep down in her heart she wanted to be saved. After I had prayed with the other people, I stood out in the hall as people were leaving. Shelly walked by, tears running down her cheeks.

"Shelly," I asked, reaching out to her, "won't you accept Jesus tonight?" She gulped and sobbed all the more. I led her to a quiet room, and there Shelly gave her heart and life to Jesus Christ.

Shelly's life is straightening out as she realized that Jesus Christ alone is her problem solver.

The Last Opportunity

One evening I was sitting at home, when the doorbell rang. Looking through our glass door, I saw a man about forty years old, dressed very mod, standing there. I opened the door. "Can I help you?"

"Yes, I'm interested in your car out here in the driveway. I noticed you have a FOR SALE sign on it."

"Sure, come on in and have a seat. I'll give you all the information about it."

It didn't take me long to work the conversation around to Jesus Christ. I shared with this man what Christ had done in my life: how He saved me, changed me, and made my life worth living. "Have you ever been saved, Dan?" I asked.

"No, I don't dig that religion bit," he replied.

"Oh, don't get me wrong, Dan," I reassured him. "I'm talking about a person—Jesus Christ—who can come into your heart to give you meaning and purpose in life so you can experience the ultimate life right here on this earth."

"Richard," Dan said slowly, "let me explain myself very, very clearly. I am glad God has changed your life. Really, I am. But it's not my bag. So I don't want to hear it any more, okay?" Then he got up to leave. "I'll be back tomorrow with the money for the car."

As Dan left, I sensed a real void in his life. I knew he needed Christ desperately because the Holy Spirit was really impressing me to keep sharing Jesus with him, even after he had made his wishes very plain to me.

Sure enough, the next day Dan came by with the money to buy my car. Since he wanted to drive it before closing the deal, we got in and went for a ride. At the prompting of the Holy Spirit, I began again to share Jesus with Dan. He became very defensive.

"Man, I told you not to put that stuff on me. I've heard it all my life." He was very nervous and edgy.

"Oh, but Dan, it's real. It's truth. Jesus changed me. And not only me, but thousands and thousands of other people have been changed, too. How can you turn down such a person as Jesus who loves you so much?"

"Richard," he said flatly, "I mean it—I don't want to hear any more about it."

Dan bought my car and drove away. It was the last time I ever saw him. Four days later he was found dead in the front seat of that car, out on a lonely, country road in northern Oklahoma. He had put a .12 gauge shotgun into his mouth, pulled the trigger, and blown off the top of his head. When I heard the news, I understood why the Holy Spirit had compelled me so strongly to share with Dan his need for salvation. Dan missed his divine appointment. God extended the call to him, but Dan rejected the love that would have saved his life forever—both on earth and in the Hereafter.

The Unwed Mothers

One day I was invited to speak at the Deaconess Home for Unwed Mothers in Oklahoma City. Several days ahead I prepared a sermon. I was really going to lay the straight, hard truth on those girls.

The time came for me to speak. I stood up and looked at the thirty-five girls, from eleven to nineteen years of age, sitting there. Suddenly I realized that the message I had prepared was inadequate. It wasn't what they needed at that moment. Their faces were sad, forlorn, forsaken. They didn't laugh or chat—they just sat there quietly staring at me.

I was at a loss for words. Not knowing how to begin, I cracked a couple of jokes. They didn't go over at all. I just did not know what to say as I looked at those empty faces, vacant eyes, swollen stomachs. Why should they trust me? I was sure that nearly every girl sitting there was the end product of listening to some boy they trusted. Some guy had whispered, "Honey, I love you, and if you love me, you'll prove it." But now the guys were gone, and the girls were left alone to pay the price.

Realizing that I couldn't keep stumbling around and searching for the right words, I asked the girls to bow their heads in prayer with me. Desperately, I asked God to give me the power, the strength at that very moment, to share the gospel with these thirty-five young ladies who were so lost and lonely.

I can hardly even remember what I said to them, but I know that God's Holy Spirit was there. He began touching hearts and working in lives. That evening four young ladies accepted Jesus as their Savior. Many more stayed after the service to talk with me and ask for prayer about family problems. They had found someone they could really trust, someone whose love for them was real and true—someone named Jesus Christ.

The Garden Club

One afternoon the president of the local ladies' garden club called and asked me to speak at their monthly meeting. One lady in the club knew that while I was in prison I had taken an eighteen-month course in horticulture. So I was to speak on that subject.

At the appointed time, I drove to the home where the garden club was meeting. Cars were everywhere. I had to park nearly half a block away. As I neared the big house, I could hear quite a lot of chatter inside. There was an unusually large crowd that evening.

Finally the meeting began and I was introduced as a lecturer on the subject of horticulture. I could hardly pronounce the word, let alone try to spell it. Even though I had taken the vocational training course in prison, I really knew very little about the subject. So I said a silent prayer, "Lord, somehow bless this whole mess." Then I got to my feet and faced the crowd of ladies. They sat smiling in anticipation.

I began by talking about plant propagation and greenhouse production. Then I told them everything I knew about growing carnations and chrysanthemums. By continuing to talk about the flowers and trees and how God loves these things, I warmed them up to topic of real importance. I told them I knew they were ladies who loved beauty, so I wanted to share the most beautiful truth that I knew: God loved them. "In fact, He loves you so much that He sent His Son, Jesus Christ, to pay the price for your sin and mine on Calvary's tree, 2,000 years ago. That's why we can receive a free pardon, we can be born again into a new realm of life. That's how I was changed from a life of crime to a life of love."

When I finished speaking, the stillness in that room was intense. I asked them all to bow their heads and pray a sinner's prayer with me if they had never been saved. The Holy Spirit was driving home the gospel to the hearts of those well-groomed, wealthy ladies. And, praise the Lord, God did what I asked Him to do—He blessed the whole mess!

"Jerry" The Escaped Convict

It was a warm summer evening and I was preaching in a meeting with Rev. Joe Morgan at South City Southern Baptist Church in Wichita, Kansas. We had almost reached the end of the meeting and it was Saturday night. God had already saved many people, but this was going to be a very special evening. A day earlier in

Oklahoma, a young man in his early twenties escaped from the state prison and caught a ride to Wichita to borrow some running money from an uncle. The uncle had heard my testimony that week and talked his nephew into meeting me at church that evening.

About a half hour before services were to begin, Jerry walked in. I knew he was in trouble. It was evident Jerry was running scared. He was very nervous and dirty; his hair was a mess; he could not sit still. The first question Jerry asked me was, "Are you going to snitch me off to the law?"

"No," I said, "I am not going to snitch you off, I just want to talk to you

I began to tell Jerry of my years of running—running from the law, running from myself, running from God.

I went on to tell Jerry how one day in prison, I ran into Jesus Christ and He changed my life. No more running now, but resting in God's peace, love, and forgiveness.

It was time to preach and Jerry sat on the last pew, as far back as he could. As I preached I prayed in my heart that Jerry would respond to the Holy Spirit's call for his life.

As we went into the invitation and began to sing "Just As I Am Without One Plea, But That Thy Blood Was Shed For Me,' several people came forward to pray with the pastor, but nc Jerry.

Another verse was sung and I kept praying for Jerry to be saved On the third verse my heart leaped with joy as Jerry stood up an began walking toward the altar. As I reached out my hand to Jerr he said, "I want to know Jesus; I need help." Praise the Lord, h was saved and a peace came over his life that evening. So muc peace that Jerry said, "I want to give myself up to the law."

The following day was Sunday and Jerry came to the mornir service. He rode back to Oklahoma with me that afternoon. C Monday afternoon we drove to El Reno where a good friend mine, Jerry Irvin, was Chief of Police. Jerry turned himself in. I had to go back to prison, but he went back in the freedom of

Christ. Jesus said, "I've come to set the captive free."

Are you running from something? Someone? Maybe God Himself? Turn yourself in to Him and you wll run no more, but walk with the Lord.

"Christians Ought to Advertise for Jesus"

If you own a Texaco station, you hang out a sign that says "Texaco". If you own a Ford dealership, you hang out a sign that says, "Ford". If you own a shoe store, you hang out a sign that says, "Shoes".

You must advertise to get results. You must get your product into the mainstream of the market.

I am a Christian and I advertise every day. Jesus is the center of my life. He is the answer to all of my questions, the solution to all of my problems. He is my Lord. So, I must tell the world about Him. I use many different methods to promote my Jesus in this dying, hell-bound world. What you are about to read is just one of many results.

In late October of 1975, I purchased an ad in the *Daily Oklahoman,* in the entertainment section, that read: "Drug Addict-Alcoholic-Prostitute-Street Freak, tired of going nowhere? Want a change? Jesus loves you and so do I, call me—Richard Coss, phone 555-4551."

Little did I know that a week earlier on October 18, God saved Kenny Colwell through a "Four Spiritual Laws" gospel tract. Kenny was in need of fellowship and discipleship, but did not know where to go. A week after his conversion he picked up a newspaper and turned to the entertainment section. Guess what was the first thing he saw? You're right; my ad. I answered my phone, "Jesus loves you." The voice on the other end said, "I've been on drugs for many years. I just accepted Jesus and I need to talk to someone; I saw your ad." I invited Kenny over to my house that evening to rap.

Kenny rode up on a 900 Kawasaki, walked to the door, and I invited him in. For a while I thought he may have trouble getting in my house, because he looked bigger than my door. He was 6'3", 270 lbs. Kenny told me his story—drugs, booze, street fighting, and concealing automatic weapons for militants. At 25 years old life had been so empty for him. Then he shared how he met Jesus Christ through a gospel tract that someone handed him. Kenny carried that tract around in his pocket for a week before reading it. He then read the scriptures in the little booklet and received Jesus Christ, as the Holy Spirit drew him.

I took Kenny on the road with me for four months, and everywhere I preached he gave his testimony. Then Kenny began to preach and I watched him grow in God's grace. He later led the girl he had been living with to faith in Christ and I had the privilege of marrying them. Today, Kenny and Debra have two beautiful daughters and, believe it or not, Kenny ministers to the needs of people in his community.

Dear brother or sister in Christ, do you advertise? Have you hung out a sign on your life that says, "Jesus Saves." "May I Help You?" "I Love You." Let's advertise our Savior.

The Good News Bus

God has allowed me to minister to hundreds of people in many areas of daily life: store clerks, gas station attendants, bartenders, prison inmates, barroom bums, policemen, and troubled boys. Wherever God leads, I go. I know there is no other life for me. And I expect great blessings from God every day. I have learned to expect His blessings, because everywhere I go, in everything I do, God continually blesses me.

The only honest profession in life I knew anything about when I left prison was tree-trimming. God led me to start my own tree-trimming and spraying business. With much hard work and His blessings, this developed into quite a busy operation. While running my business in Oklahoma City, I also worked with the

Larry Jones Evangelistic Association. It was not just mere coincidence that brought Larry and I together.

One day, several months after I had accepted Jesus in the penitentiary, Larry Jones came to our prison for a three-day crusade. He had a powerful, persuasive way of talking about God. This was the first real preaching I'd ever heard in my life. One evening after the service, I talked with him. "Larry, God has been dealing with me concerning your work. After I'm released from this place, if they permit me to parole in Oklahoma City, I'll be glad to help you or work with you in any way."

Sure enough, upon my release I went to see Larry Jones. He put me to work. I helped him in many tent crusades, from Texas to Oregon to Kentucky, sharing my testimony with thousands and thousands of people. For four years I worked part-time with Larry in crusades.

Also at this time, God placed a burden on my heart for the hundreds of hitchhikers I saw along the highways we traveled. Whenever I have room in my car, I always pick up hitchhikers. I get to share Christ with them as long as I want to, for their time is really at my disposal. After all, when we're whizzing down the highway, they're not likely to jump out, so they are a captive audience for the gospel!

In this way I have seen several hitchhikers come to know Jesus. It is such a simple method of ministry. God kept dealing with me to initiate a ministry to hitchhikers. The more I prayed about it, the heavier this burden became. Finally, I shared the concept with several close Christian friends. We prayed about it together, and we felt the release in the Spirit to go ahead and develop the ministry.

Thus, the Good News Bus came into being. The bus would be a ministry to hitchhikers along the Oklahoma interstate highways. It would be a part-time ministry for all of us who had several spare hours a week to drive the bus and pick up hitchhikers. The only catch was that we didn't have a bus.

So, I began to look for something suitable. One day I came upon

a 1964, eight-door Checker, which had been an airport limousine.
"What will you sell it for?" I asked the car salesman.
"Seventeen hundred," he replied tersely.
"What's your bottom dollar?"
"Seventeen. Not a penny less. It'll bring that," he assured me
between chomps on his cigar and puffs of smoke.
"Can I see how it drives?" I asked.
"Sure," he said, grinning and pitching the key to me. "Hop in."
It was in good running condition, and seemed to meet our
needs perfectly. "I'll take it," I told the man. "Just hold it for me
until tomorrow, and I'll be back to pick it up." I had five dollars in
my pocket at the time.

That evening I called several Christian businessmen who knew
about this burden on my heart. I described the bus to them and
then asked for their financial help. The next day I took the $300
they had given me to the salesman. "This is a deposit," I told him.
"You let me have the bus, and I'll get you the balance of the $1,700
by next week."

He let me take the limousine. And the next week $1,400 came
in the mail to pay it off.

We began the ministry. The first order of business was to get
the bus painted—a bright red, white, and blue. On the side was
painted "Good News Bus." We put Jesus stickers on the windows,
"One Way" fingers pointing upward on the back, and scripture
verses of the Roman road to salvation on the side doors. I
thought when I saw it in all its finished glory that the old Checker
itself had been reborn. It was a message in itself.

Sometimes we had as many as ten hitchhikers riding in that
limousine. We gave them peanut butter sandwiches and Gideon
New Testaments. Food for their bodies and for their souls. We
also kept an ample supply of tracts to give them. In the two years
of part-time ministry to hitchhikers, thirteen men accepted Jesus
as their personal Savior. We know that five of them today are still
serving the Lord.

One of the first young men we picked up was a seventeen-year-old runaway from Tulsa. His hair was just long enough to curl down over his collar, and his scraggly beard was barely getting started. His name was Mike. He was headed for California—the runaways' so-called "promised land."

"I'm gonna find a new thing, get turned on. Find life," he said.

We headed on down the road. I casually remarked, "You know, Mike, you can find new life right here in this bus. Right there where you're sitting you can get turned on to a real, true, meaningful life."

"What are you talking about, man?" he asked, puzzled. So I told him. For thirty miles I shared Jesus with him. Finally, I pulled onto the shoulder and led Mike to an experience with Jesus Christ. Right there on Interstate 40 Mike found the new life he had run away to seek.

I had to take care of some business in a city off the highway, so I let Mike out. But first I asked him to pray about his decision to go to California, to ask the Lord what to do. My business took about an hour, after which I headed back the way I had come. As I came back onto the interstate heading eastward for Oklahoma City, there stood Mike by the side of the road, thumb out, grinning from ear to ear. He climbed back into the bus. "Man, I've already had a round with the devil, and I won!" he laughed. "Old devil said to cut on out to California, but the Lord told me to go back home to my folks. Tulsa, here I come."

Mike did go home. He reconciled with his parents, finished school, eventually married, and now has a family of his own. He's still living for Jesus. During the two years with the Good News Bus, scores of others like Mike heard the message of life and love. Some received it; some went on their way. But all were touched by the warmth of that divine moment when they trucked down I-40 in God's Good News Bus.

El Reno Prison
for Jesus

During all this time, my tree-trimming and spraying business became secondary to the Lord's work. On many days my equipment just sat idle in the driveway while I was out preaching somewhere and sharing my faith in Christ. I knew that if I kept my eyes on Jesus first and others second, I didn't have to worry about finances. He would take care of me. That's the deal we have between us, and it has always worked.

Then came the day the Lord told me to sell the business, to go into full-time work for Him. Pastor John Lucas of Sunnylane Baptist Church in Del City, Oklahoma, called me about coming to his church as Associate Pastor and Youth Director. It was so miraculous to see God's leading in my life, for I had met Brother John at a revival meeting the very night I was paroled from prison. I was asked to live my testimony in the service there. Brother John and his lovely wife, Helen, heard me, came over after the meeting to introduce themselves, and then took me out for a late snack so we could get better acquainted. Now here he was, two years later, calling me to work together with him!

It was to be two years of learning, growing closer to the Lord and His people, and having varied, wonderful experiences.

Like the time we went back to El Reno.

Early in 1974, the chaplain at the El Reno Prison called, inviting me to bring our youth group and hold a service for the inmates. I gladly accepted, eager for the opportunity to have young people share their faith. We spent a week in prayer preparing our hearts for the night of ministry. The young people were excited, expecting a great move of God.

That Sunday afternoon we loaded our sound equipment on the church bus and headed for El Reno, thirty-five miles away. I drove the bus. The kids gathered in different groups to pray. I particularly remember one group asking the Lord to move at least twelve inmates to make decisions for Christ. That number was significant.

The service began. The young people played their instruments, sang their messages, and told their testimonies. Then they sat in silent prayer the whole time I was ministering to the prisoners. At the time of invitation, seven inmates immediately came forward. I asked them to stand quietly while others considered their souls' eternal destinies. Soon three more inmates walked to the front and joined the seven. I could almost hear the young people pleading, "Two more, Lord. We asked for at least twelve."

At the end of the invitational song, nineteen inmates had come forward. Twelve of them had decided to give their hearts and lives to Jesus. You talk about some excited young people.

We serve not only a soul-saving and problem-solving God, but our Lord is a prayer-answering God in the people-loving business. I praise Him that nothing such as bars, walls, wires, guntowers, or solid concrete can stop the power of the Holy Spirit. He goes to the darkest holes of despair to draw men and women to Jesus.

Lenita

I enjoyed working with the young people of Sunnylane. Each Sunday I looked forward to another great day with the Lord and His people. One Sunday morning as I pulled into the church parking lot, I noticed a young girl sitting alone in her car. It was Lenita Levan. I had tried to get acquainted with her before, but she was very withdrawn. Every time I tried to talk to her, I carried on a one-sided conversation. She would only mumble one or two words and would never look me in the face. I knew Lenita was on drugs.

"No use trying again," I told myself. "She already resents me." So I started to the sanctuary. Before I got there, the Holy Spirit spoke within me clearly. "Richard, go back to Lenita and tell her again about Jesus' love for her and about His power to save her and deliver her. She is ready to listen. I have prepared her heart."

I whirled around, raced back to her car, and got in beside her. Just as the Holy Spirit had instructed, I began to share Jesus and His saving power with this shy, sad girl. In a few minutes Lenita bowed her head, confessed her sins, and believed in Jesus Christ as Lord. When she looked up straight into my eyes, her face was glowing. We could almost hear the angels rejoicing as they wrote her name in Heaven's Book of Life.

A few days later Lenita, with a group of our young people, held a "flush service" at a prayer meeting. Lenita flushed all her drugs down the commode, out of her life forever. One week later she threw fourteen packs of cigarettes in the garbage. "That's where they belong," she declared.

The Lord had truly changed Lenita. Since she was a new creature in Christ, she was no longer withdrawn. In fact, she began to reach out to lost souls, witnessing and passing out tracts. She was soon baptized, and she became a great worker within the church. Later she enrolled in a Christian college. Today, Lenita lives to tell others who have not heard about her Savior.

Not long after her life was so dramatically changed, Lenita handed me this poem she had written:

> There's a man in our church, We call him "Big Red"
> Because of the color of his big, bushy head.
> This man is special to the lives of many people,
> For oft he will counsel and show them the steeple.
> When this man is happy the whole church can tell,
> Cause he'll have a smile so wonderfully swell.
> But this man is nothing without Christ the Savior,
> Who died on the cross—what a wonderful favor!
> Christ can change men, like "Big Red" and me,
> Why don't you trust Him and from sin be set free?

This simple little poem is precious to me because it is the outpouring of a heart filled by the love of Jesus.

The Funeral

After nearly two great years at Sunnylane, the Lord began to prepare me for a change. I didn't know what was around the corner, but if it was as good as what was on this side, I was ready for it. I resigned the position at Sunnylane to preach revival meetings.

Toward the end of summer, I received a call from Trinity Baptist Church in Weatherford, Oklahoma. A deacon on the other end of the line was asking if I would consider becoming their pastor? That was quite a big step for me to take, although I had already been ordained. I prayed about this for several weeks. Finally, I received a definite confirmation in my spirit. This was the path God had directed. I moved to Weatherford.

As an ordained minister, I performed several wedding ceremonies. I found it an enjoyable part of my ministry. Of course, I always counseled the couple and shared Christ with them. Weddings came easily.

However, I had never been called upon to conduct a funeral. Sometimes I wondered what I would say when I was asked to do so—as I inevitably would be some day. That day was not long in coming. And it seemed to me that God let me have the toughest job of all. It was not a dear, sweet old saint who had slipped on home to glory. No; it was the absolute contrary.

A friend of mine called late one night to tell me that her brother had just been shot and killed in a barroom brawl. She asked me to preach the funeral. "I don't know, Pam," I told her honestly. "I'll pray about it and do whatever the Lord tells me to do." That seemed to satisfy her. Evidently she had already asked the Lord about it.

On my knees, I sought the Lord. "Why this one, Lord? I do not know if the young man was saved. What can I say?"

The answer came as clear as a bell on a still night: "You can share Jesus with the living who come to honor the dead."

When Pam called back the next morning, I said, "Yes, Pam, I'll preach your brother's funeral."

The funeral chapel was filled with the young man's friends. The barmaids, the go-go girls, the bartenders, his drinking buddies—they were all there. What a congregation! After giving some basic facts about the young man's life, I turned my attention to the lost ones before me. Sharing my testimony and preaching the gospel, I could see their attention riveted on me. This was like no funeral they had ever been to. Me either!

After I had finished, I gave an invitation.

Thirteen people accepted Jesus as their Savior! Praise God. What more consolation could you want at a funeral than knowing that thirteen names were written down in the Lamb's Book of Life?

Actually, after I considered it, there is no better time to preach the gospel than at a funeral. People's minds are focused suddenly on the question of eternal life. As I think back to my own father's funeral, I remember that the minister didn't say one thing about Jesus. He just recounted how my father was a good man, completely glossing over the fact of my father's alcoholism, his family problems, his fussing and fighting, and his unregenerate son. In fact, he didn't really even tell the truth. If he had, I might have been saved that day. Perhaps others would have accepted Jesus, too. But we weren't given the opportunity. Nobody heard the gospel that day. A lady did sing, "The Old Rugged Cross", but I guessed it was some kind of Marine Corps hymn, since my father was receiving a Marine Corps burial.

During all those years I was in sin. I can never remember attending one funeral where the gospel was preached. Looking back, it seems like wasted effort—not sharing Jesus at a funeral. I believe every funeral I ever preach will be a time of sharing the gospel. That's the reason the Lord handed me such a tough first one: to set the pattern for all those to come.

George Harmon

Because of my past life and conversion, I have a special burden in my heart for prison inmates. To this day I use every opportunity I get to speak in jails and prisons around the country. Once I went into the Federal Prison in Sandstone, Minnesota. As I walked through the gate, I spotted George Harmon, my handicapped companion of years ago, running toward me on crutches. "Hi, Richard," he greeted me. "How are you, man? What are you doing here? Why did they bust you?"

I laughed joyously. "Man I didn't get busted. I got saved! I'm here to preach a revival!" George's eyes nearly popped out of their sockets.

George came to the revival every night. He sat in the back row of the chapel with his head bowed low. Each night I expected him to decide for Jesus. Each night I was disappointed. The meeting was about to end when I confronted him. "George, what are you going to do with Jesus?"

He shook his head. "I can't Rich. I can't do it."

"Man, you need to be saved!" I pleaded.

"I know it, but I can't." He had a haunted, scared look in his eyes. "You don't understand, Rich. I'm in organized crime now, in way over my head. If I get right with God and God changes my life, the big guys would think I'm a snitch or a turncoat. I'm afraid they would kill me."

I continued to pray for George's salvation, and I corresponded with him weekly, encouraging him to accept God's new life. He soon gave his life to Christ. Praise the Lord!

I have found that people behind bars listen to what I have to say. I'm sure it is because I've sat where they sit. I have rapport with them. I use their lingo. And I have seen many lives changed, many people saved during the time of invitation in jails and prisons. I am thankful that God is moving in this area.

Mom

Another burden I carry is for the alcoholic. Alcoholism contributed greatly to my father's death in 1963, and it has drained the life from my mother. When I left prison, one of the first persons in my family that I witnessed to was my mom. As I shared Christ with her, she became very defensive. She claimed to be a Catholic, but she never attended mass.

Each summer I would go back to share Christ with her. One day as I witnessed to her, she lost her temper, cursed me, ordered me out of her house, and told me I was no longer her son. But I knew God was dealing in her heart and life. I believed by faith my mother was going to be saved. Jesus told us, "Ask, and ye shall receive." I asked for my mother's acceptance of Jesus as her Savior. She was saved in 1979. Praise the Lord!

One day I went back to the bar in Danbury, Wisconsin, where my mother had worked when I was five years old. I could hardly believe my eyes. I saw the same people sitting on the same barstools that were there twenty-five years ago. They've been there all these years—drinking. The tragedy of it all—the wasted years, the empty lives. No meaning, no purpose, no joy, no desire, nothing but that bottle. They are drinking their lives away, slowly being devoured by Satan's bottle.

I have tried to share Christ with many of the people I knew as a little boy, but they are very indifferent to the gospel. Perhaps they're afraid it will upset their lives. Or maybe their pride is too strong for them to admit after fifty years that they've been wrong.

Many, many times God leads me to saloons and bars to witness. As I share Christ with the people there, I never condemn them. I tell them I love them and offer a better way of life than spending the rest of their days on a barstool drinking their lives away, as surely bound by Satan as if they were wrapped in chains.

I have seen men and women both bow their heads right there

at the bar, pray a sinner's prayer, and accept Christ as their Savior. I've met others outside headed in for a night of boozing and seen them bow their heads as they stood right there at the door. I've watched as they accepted Christ, then turned away from the door of temptation and went yon, a new person in Jesus. You know, God really does still perform miracles today. He turns beer, cigarettes, and whiskey into food, furniture, and clothing. I've seen him do it!

After my mother became a Christian she said, "Son, if I die before you do, I want you to preach my funeral. And be sure to preach Jesus."

My mother went home to glory in the spring of 1985. I preached Jesus.

"See you later, Mom."

The Boys Ranch

In 1978 God called me to build and direct the "Christ Bars None Boys Ranch" in Noble, Oklahoma. I directed that ministry for almost seven years, until God said: "I need you somewhere else now, get ready to move."

Those seven years were good years. We saw over 200 boys come and go. Most of them gave their lives to Jesus Christ. Here are a few examples.

Almost every boy at the Ranch had experienced personal tragedy and injury. Two brothers, "Don and Jim" (names changed), were given money for a movie and left at a shopping mall. Their mother never returned for them.

Eleven-year-old "Phillip" came because his mother was dying from cancer. Without any other relatives, "Phillip" would soon be alone except for his Christian family at the ranch.

Gang member "Brannon" was 16 when he was busted for selling drugs in Missouri. Then, a jail chaplain led him to the Lord. To prevent his testimony, the other gang members promised to kill him. The chaplain was my personal friend and he sent "Brannon" here to save his life.

"Dewey" was 15 when he was sent to a state institution for evaluation. In his second week there, he was homosexually raped by the other patients. His mother and social worker then sent him to the ranch. Here he found a Christian atmosphere of love.

"Roger" was a preacher's son. He was burglarizing homes for drug money. When he was 14, he pointed a .38 special right at a man's heart and pulled the trigger. Fortunately, the gun misfired.

Nine-year-old "David" was sexually abused by his stepfathers. An alcoholic mother neglected him and resented his interference with her lifestyle. Days would pass when "David" and his brother didn't see their often suicidal mother.

"Jack's" stepfather is in prison. His stepfather was a prison escapee who got saved and then turned himself in. "Jack's" mother couldn't make it financially for her large family without her husband, so "Jack" came to us. But in a few months, their Christian family was reunited.

These are just a sample of the reasons boys came to us. Besides working with the boys, we provided a Christian psychologist to counsel and witness to the parents. If a boy was going to go home again, we wanted him to go home to a Christian home.

First Bank of Heaven

Give what you've got—to get what you want—a Spiritual law!

God said in Malachi, "You thieves and robbers, you are cursed because you have stolen from me." Was God speaking to the lost? No, He was speaking to His children. "Give and it shall be given unto you, good measure, pressed down, shaken together, running over, for with the same measure that you measure it shall be measured unto you." God says unto you and me today, as He did then, "Prove me, and see if I will not open for you the windows of Heaven, and pour out for you a blessing, that there shall not be room enough to receive it."

How much have you given to the storehouse of God that others might have food, clothing, shelter and spiritual blessings? The Bible teaches you and me, the more we give the more we get to give.

I began tithing and giving in 1969 while making the huge sum of $15 a month in the El Reno Prison. I had never been a giver, always a taker. Giving was not my nature. But now I possessed a new nature, a giving nature that God put in me. Today, Phyllis and I are able to give more to His work than a lot of people make each year. And God's financial blessings keep coming in to take care of both our needs and the needs of others.

I believe Christians are receiving and distribution stations. What God has given to us we are to give away to others. We cannot out-give God. Remember, He said, "Prove Me and I will fill your barns to overflowing." Not only did He promise to fill our barns, He also promised to rebuke the devourer for our sakes. Hallelujah, the teeth of the old roaring lion Satan have been pulled out back at Calvary.

Jesus said, "I am come that you might have life and have it more abundantly." Soul winners and givers live more abundantly than anyone I know. You should be living like a King's Kid. Remember, God has said, "It is greater to give than to receive." If God's Word is true, let's do what he said.

Let's give because we love Him.

CHAPTER 12

Pardoned

One afternoon in September 1974, my good friend Gil Burk, asked me to testify at a campaign meeting with him. Gil was running for the State Office of Charities and Corrections, since he has a burden for prison inmates and a desire to help them.

As we drove that evening to Lawton, Oklahoma, Gil asked, "Are you going to vote for me, Richard?"

"Gil, you know I have no voting rights. I'm an ex-con, remember?"

"Oh, yes, that's right. Sometimes I forget," he said, flashing me a smile. He was silent for a moment, thinking. At last he asked, "Richard, have you ever considered asking for a pardon from the President of the United States?"

"Yes, I've thought about it. But, you know, since I've already received a pardon from the King, Jesus Christ, I have decided to leave the other pardon up to Him. If He wants me to have a Presidential Pardon restoring my civil rights, the Lord will see to it in due time."

"Richard, I believe it's time to start praying about it," Gil said.

So Gil and I, along with several other friends, began to seek God's will in this matter. Immediately doors began to open. I discovered that since I had been out of prison four years already, I was now eligible for a Presidential Pardon and executive clemency.

I wrote a letter to the President's Pardon Attorney in Washington, D.C., sharing my testimony with him. He sent me all the necessary forms to fill out. This process took about two weeks, since many of the forms were character references to be completed by other people. Finally they were all completed and returned to the Pardon Attorney.

Then an extensive FBI investigation began. One evening I was having a prayer meeting at my house, when the doorbell rang. At the door stood a young, very professional FBI agent. He flashed his ID and badge. "Come with me, please," he directed. It was like a scene out of my past, but this time it was just an interview about the pardon.

Down at the headquarters, the agent studied my long rap-sheet of 32 arrests. Finally, he asked, "What's been keeping you out of trouble for the past four years?"

"Jesus," I replied simply.

He glanced at me, startled. Then asked, "Just why do you want this pardon?"

"Mainly because it would open more doors for me to serve God and my country." I could almost see the agent's thoughts: "Why would an ex-con with so many arrests on his record now want to contribute to society?" I just smiled the love of Jesus at him.

The agent then went to ask my Parole Officer, Charles Pippin, whether or not I was for real. He wasn't prepared for the fact that Charlie is a born-again believer in the Lord Jesus Christ. Charlie unloaded on him, too. In fact, everyone that FBI agent went to see gave him the same, simple story: "Jesus saves and changes lives. Richard is living proof."

After two months, the FBI finally completed their investigation. Their report was sent to the Pardon Attorney to be forwarded to President Ford.

On December 23, 1975, Richard David Coss received a full and unconditional pardon from the President of the United States, Gerald R. Ford.

On January 15, 1976, Richard David Coss received from the Department of Justice a Warrant of Executive Clemency.

His full rights have been restored!

(Isaiah 5:57)

Now, therefore, be it known, that Gerald R. Ford, President of the United States of America, in consideration of the premises, diverse other good and sufficient reasons, has granted unto the said Richard David Coss a full and unconditional pardon and designated, directed and empowered the Attorney General as his representative to sign this grant of Executive Clemency.

In accordance with these instructions and authority I have signed my name and caused the seal of the Department of Justice to be affixed below and affirm that this action is the act of the President being performed at his direction.

Done at the City of Washington this twenty-third day of December in the year of our Lord One Thousand Nine Hundred and seventy-five and of the Independence of the United States the Two Hundredth.

By direction of the President

Edward H. Levi
Attorney General

United States Department of Justice
Office of the Pardon Attorney
Washington, D.C. 20530
Dec. 23, 1975

Honorable Dewey Bartlett
United States Senator
215 N.W. 3rd Street
Suite 812
Oklahoma City, Oklahoma 73102

Dear Senator Bartlett:

This refers to your interest in Richard David Coss.

On the above date, the President granted Mr. Coss of Del City, Oklahoma a full and unconditional pardon.

Sincerely,

Lawrence M. Traylor
Pardon Attorney

Office of the Attorney General
Washington, D.C. 20530
Jan. 15, 1976

Mr. Richard David Coss
of Del City, Oklahoma 73115

Dear Mr. Coss:

It gives me great pleasure to transmit to you a warrant signifying that President Ford has granted you a full and unconditional pardon.

The grant of a federal pardon is an extraordinary act of grace which only the President may confer and which represents his determination of your fitness. In this way, the President recognizes that by observance of high moral standards you are worthy of the forgiveness which the pardon symbolizes.

President Ford has asked me to convey to you his best wishes for the future and to express his confidence that in the years to come you will continue to merit the trust that he has placed in you.

Sincerely,

Edward H. Levi
Attorney General

DEPARTMENT of JUSTICE

Washington, __January 15, 1976__

TO: __Richard David Coss__
__P.O. Box 15436__
__Del City, Oklahoma 73155__

SIR:

Herewith receive Warrant __of Executive__

__clemency__

By direction of the Attorney General.

Very respectfully,

Lawrence M. Traylor
Lawrence M. Traylor
Pardon Attorney

CHAPTER 13

Divorced
But Not Disqualified

To those of you reading this not-so-nice chapter of my life who have been through or are going through the pain, hurt, and anguish of a divorce will feel and understand what I am writing. Others will not and I hope you never will. Some will twist the scripture around to say, "Brother, you're out of the ministry" or "God cannot use a divorced person" and even, "Dear sister, we have no place for you in our church any longer." My own personal experience with divorce and my church was very sad and painful.

Having been called into the ministry for 16 years, and being a staff member at one of Oklahoma's largest churches for 10 years, I had the freedom to be an evangelist. I preached Jesus everywhere I went. I preached messages on marriage and family relationships every week. The Holy Spirit used me many times to give counsel to troubled marriages. I hated divorce and still do. I believe divorce is a sin; the Word says it is. But like any other sin, divorce is a forgiveable sin. Still, divorce leaves you devastated. It left me devastated and terribly down. But God said, "Richard, I have chosen you, I have called you, so get up, for my callings and elections are without repentance and I will never leave you or forsake you." Praise God for the healing power of the Word.

It was 1985. I had just finished preaching a week-long revival in a small town in northern Oklahoma. It was a beautiful Sunday evening and I was making a three hour drive home. As I drove, my mind was reflecting back over the week's decisions. Fifteen people had accepted Christ as their Lord. Others had gained victory over problems and grew in the faith. It was a good week and I was just praising the Lord as I drove home. I lived seventeen miles east of Norman, Oklahoma, out in the country. As I turned my Ford pickup into my driveway I noticed something different. When you have lived someplace for ten years you can tell when things are not the same. My two dogs came running up to me, jumping all over me, and barking happily. I saw one of the cats sitting on the front porch and I noticed the horses out by the barn, but things still were not right. I stepped up on the front porch, opened the door, and walked into my home, flipping on the light switch.

Light revealed what I feared in the darkness. I no longer had a home; only an empty house. My wife of fifteen years was gone, the kids were gone, and every piece of furniture in that six-bedroom, five-bathroom, 4,000-square-foot house was gone. I ran through the house but no one was there except me. I found an old, worn-out mattress she had left behind, pulled it down to my bedroom, laid down, and cried all night.

The next morning my good friend, Harold Bittick, came by to spend the day with me. We talked and prayed and prayed and talked. As we walked out of the house to feed the horses in the barn, Harold noticed something and he turned to me. "Richard," he said, "the only thing left behind are the nail holes in the walls where the pictures once hung. That reminds me of Jesus and His nail holes where He once hung." I needed that, and I have never forgotten it. Jesus hung and hurt for me. He suffered all things for me. He's been there—now, comfort me Jesus.

Three days later my children called and said "Come and get us dad." I am sure my Ford pickup broke a few speed laws that day, but, I was in a hurry. As I drove up to a rented house, Danny and Edye were standing in the doorway with their bags packed. We hugged and kissed each other and headed home. Oh, how God used Danny and Edye in my life to help me keep my sanity.

As we drove up to our house Edye said, "Well Dad, we live in the biggest house in the country. We just don't have any furniture." She laughed and then looked over at the swimming pool, saying, "Dad, we could go swimming this afternoon but we don't have any towels to dry off with." She laughed again. She was thirteen at the time. I prayed for her little broken heart and she ministered to her dad.

Danny is my adopted son and what a cut-up he is. Later that night I said, "Okay kids let's go to bed." Danny said, "What beds? We don't have any. It's a good thing I brought my sleeping bag." Danny was eleven when we adopted him, he was sixteen when the divorce came. I know both of them were hurting inside. It didn't show up at home, but it did at school. Their grades dropped, Edye got into a couple of fights, and was suspended for three days. We kept praying and things got better.

I belonged to a church that enrolled 4,000 in Sunday School. I was a staff member for ten years and was in charge of their Prison Ministry and Boys Ranch. I had hundreds of close friends within that fellowship. When the word got out that my wife had left and was getting a divorce, only six people called or came by to see me during the next ten months.

I have learned a lot about ministering to the divorced person since then. They all need friends and someone from the church to love them. They need phone calls and letters, reassuring them of God's forgiveness and God's help in times of trouble. They need to be invited out to eat and over for fellowship. We do not need to take sides on who was right or wrong. We must unconditionally love them and help them get back to a normal life.

Sometimes we must help them financially. We had a new pastor at our church and he told me I needed to move on. I was the father of two children and broke. Divorce sometimes leaves a person in debt. I had no money, no furniture, very little food in the house, and owed a $4,000 attorney fee. I did not make a house payment for ten months. One of my best friends and a brother in Christ, Dr. Sam Cornelius, gave me $1,000 during this time. Another friend, J.B. Askins, gave me $400. Two pastors who heard I was divorced called and cancelled our meetings. Five other pastors said, "We love you brother, come and preach for us." Praise God for loving, giving, and forgiving believers!

A pastor friend of mine made this statement at a men's conference: "Husband, don't divorce your wife, kill her. Baptists will forgive you for murder." He went on to say, "You will go to prison for a few years and pay your debt to society. When you leave prison you will be a widower and you can scripturally remarry." Unfortunately there is a lot of truth to that statement.

The kids and I were trusting God for everything and He kept coming through every day to meet our needs. Their grades were picking up at school. We were laughing more and becoming a family again. God gave me the help I needed to be a single parent, and man did I ever need help. Even though my kids and I had always spent a lot of time together, I was now learning what the word "Father" meant.

Both Danny and Edye were basketball players at their schools, so we always had a game to go to, and their friends from school were always hanging out at our house. As a matter of fact, Edye had a swimming pool party and fifty-three teenagers showed up. I have never grilled so many hot dogs in my life but it was great fun. Most importantly of all, we led a girl to Jesus that night, but that was nothing new since kids were witnessed to every week around our house. Danny and Edye were both Christians. All their friends knew it and respected them.

In spite of the divorce, we were all climbing on to higher ground in our Christian walk. We always had a lot of love for each other and the three favorite words in our vocabulary are "I love you." Those are miracle words with a lot of healing in them.

Dear Christian friend; how long will we continue to judge and disqualify for service the divorced Christian? Do you remember the old Indian proverb, "Do not judge me unless you have walked ten miles in my moccasins?" I am so glad we can count on the Lamb of God who takes away the sins of the world. Divorce included!

CHAPTER 14

Remarriage—Phyllis's Story

I had resolved in my own mind that I would remain a single parent. I was not out and about looking for a wife. I was still recovering and recuperating from the emotional pain and scars of divorce, but I knew with the help of the Word and the Holy Spirit Comforter I would prevail.

In the late spring of 1986, my good friend Mike Story, former pastor of Angus Acres Baptist Church in Sand Springs, Oklahoma, had me in for a week-long evangelistic meeting. This was my eighth meeting with Mike in ten years. Angus Acres runs about five hundred in Sunday School. Not bad, considering that in 1980 they averaged only forty-five in Sunday School.

It was during that week of preaching and ministering to the needs of the people that I met Phyllis. She was the pastor's secretary. As a matter of fact, she was the most unusual pastor's secretary I had ever met. I had heard about Phyllis for four years. She was the talk of Tulsa, Oklahoma. Organized crime talked about Phyllis, drug addicts talked about Phyllis, nightclub owners talked about Phyllis, policemen talked about Phyllis, and pastors who came into Mike Story's office talked about Phyllis. I believe the best way for me to describe Phyllis to you is to let her tell her own story.

Personal Testimony of
Phyllis Louise Coss

At the age of thirteen I busted loose from my parents and hit the streets. At thirteen I did what I had to do to survive in my environment. I hung out with a party crowd that was mostly older than I. After a couple of years on the streets and knowing the right people it was easy to get fake ID's. Looking much older than I actually was made it easy to walk in and out of the Tulsa nightclubs. I drank, partied, and fought almost every night. As a matter of fact, if I didn't have a fight before I went home at night I thought I had missed something. At 130 pounds I was stronger than most other women. While growing up I had learned where to hit another person and how to hurt them.

If my fists and feet did not work for me, the loaded .38 special in my purse did. By the 1960s the Tulsa police knew me well. I had already made my mark in the city and county jail. I had no fear of jail, since I usually made bail before they got the paperwork done. Besides, most of the other women in jail were friends of mine from the streets. During the early years I went to jail for public drunk, hot checks, assault, vagrancy, and shoplifting.

Occasionally I had twenty-five or thirty days in the county jail, and was always the hero at the nightclubs when I got out. It was party time again! One night, while driving home drunk, I passed out at the wheel and hit another car head-on. The driver was killed instantly. The policeman in charge knew me from the clubs and liked me. I was ticketed for negligent homicide but not drunk driving. In other words he let me walk. I received a one year probation.

As I grew older I also grew wiser. I began to notice other things besides alcohol, dope, and men. I began to notice what I thought the finer things of life consisted of: Lincolns, Cadillacs, big diamonds, and silk dresses. I just had to have those things in my possession, but I knew I could not afford these luxuries of life by writing hot checks, shoplifting, bartending, and robbing drunken men in some sleazy bar or motel room.

I got the word out I wanted in on some real action—big money action. Tulsa criminals already knew me, and I was known as "good people," not an undercover agent or snitch. It wasn't long before the "Funny Money People" made contact with me one night at a club.

Making, delivering, selling, and cashing counterfeit money became my new profession. I have seen times when the trunk of my Cadillac would hardly close because of all the "funny money" in it. The luxuries of life I thought I just had to have became mine. To go to the most exclusive stores in Tulsa and buy $300 silk blouses and $400 silk dresses, fur coats, and leather coats was no problem. I had twenty-five pairs of expensive shoes and leather boots in my closet. Diamond rings were on every finger and diamond studs were in my ears. I just loved "things," and I had them. It was the best clothing stores, restaurants, and clubs for me. I thought I was fulfilled and happy. Little did I know that God, in His great grace, love, and mercy had a wonderful plan for my life. God was closing in on me but so was the FBI.

"Don't do the crime if you can't do the time." I'd heard sayings like that most of my life and I knew the consequences of living on the other side of the law. Sure enough, the FBI closed in on us and busted the ring. Back to the county jail to await trial in federal court.

The FBI had me. I pled guilty and the good judge saw fit to give me ten years in federal prison. I was sent to the Alderson Federal Womens Prison in Alderson, West Virginia.

The judge gave me an A-2 sentence, which meant I could parole early. I did—six months later. I walked through the prison gates, caught a train and headed for "Tulsa town." It was back to the bars, the clubs, and the old way of life. I still had my diamonds and all of my silk wardrobe. I was soon back in business—counterfeit money. The love of Jesus was still trying to reach me, but I ran. God was after me and so was the FBI. The latter caught me first, and back I went to Alderson Federal Prison. On this stretch I pulled two years and three months.

During those years of criminal activity I gave birth to two

beautiful little girls, Pam and Kim. I stopped my life of partying just long enough to go to the hospital and have my babies. I was not a good mother. I wanted to party and do crime so I gave my little babies to my mother and father to raise. The worst thing I remember about prison was that once a month, for five minutes, you were allowed to call home. I would call my mother and she would put my two little girls on the phone. As soon as they heard their mother's voice they would start crying and they'd cry the whole five minutes. It was heartbreaking to listen to my little girls cry for five minutes every month for twenty-seven months. Needless to say, I came out of prison harder and colder than when I went in.

After I did my twenty-seven months I made parole, caught the train back to "Tulsa town," and moved in with my mom, dad, and two daughters. I kept a low profile for a while. I was really trying to stay out of trouble this time. After several weeks with my family, it was time to hit the streets again. Something inside was drawing me back to the old life, back to the world I knew so well.

My dad is a deacon in the Presbyterian church who loves Jesus Christ and souls. He tried to talk to me and warn me, but again I did not listen. This time I went into professional shoplifting, stealing only the best of women's silk clothing. In my little black book were the names and phone numbers of doctors' wives, lawyers' wives, polticians' wives, and dozens of others who bought my hot clothes for one half the sticker price. Professional shoplifting took me from Tulsa to Memphis and Little Rock, then back to Tulsa. The next trip would be to Los Angeles and back, shoplifting my way through each city. Every few days I would package up all of my hot clothes and send them by UPS back to Tulsa for safekeeping until I returned. I bought a house in a nice subdivision in Sand Springs, Oklahoma. I had a brand new Oldsmobile Toronado sitting in the driveway. Again things looked good. I had my parties, I had my diamonds, I had my silk clothes.

It was June of 1981 and God began closing in on me. His Holy Spirit was knocking on my door. I was going through a divorce. My husband was a heroin addict and had been in prison three times.

He broke my jaw and had shot at me during a fight. I had to get out. He went back to prison and I got my divorce. I was depressed, lonely, and searching for something. I walked my little toy-poodle every day. I lived at the end of a cul-de-sac and only had one way to walk my dog. Every day the lady in the corner house would see me coming with my dog and she would come out to tell me about Jesus Christ. Day after day, week after week, she faithfully witnessed to me about the saving grace of Jesus. She invited me to her church and I finally decided to go with her.

On June 6, 1981, at Angus Acres Baptist Church, I gave it all to Jesus. My heart, my life, all of my worldly possessions. I needed Him and He wanted me. I became a Christian. Angus Acres is a disciple-making church and I was their new disciple. I went through Evangelism Explosion, and through the power of the Holy Spirit I became a soul-winner. I have always had a big mouth, but now I was His spokeswoman—telling others of God's love and forgiveness. Then I went through Master Life, another disciple-making program. Two years later I became the pastor's secretary.

Today I have a wonderful relationship with my two daughters, (and two grandchildren). My mom has gone home with Jesus and my dad still loves Him. And by the way, I married the redheaded evangelist who came to my church in 1986. We have a lot in common. We both love the Lord Jesus, we love His Word, we love the Holy Spirit's work in our lives, and we love the ministry God has given us.

In closing, Habakkuk 3:17-19 says it all for me: "Even though the fig trees have no fruit and no grapes grow on the vines, even though the olive crop fails and the fields produce no grain, even though the sheep all die and the cattle stalls are empty, I will still be joyful and glad, because the Lord God is my savior. The Sovereign Lord gives me strength. He makes me sure-footed as a deer and keeps me safe on the mountains."

Love in Christ,
Phyllis L. Coss

CHAPTER 15

Final Thoughts

Well, as you can see, God had different plans for me. At a time when I thought I would never fall in love again, Phyllis came into my life. It was a brand new beginning for all of us—Phyllis, myself, and my two children. Today Phyllis and I serve Christ together as husband and wife in full-time evangelism. Dear reader, I want you to know that God is a God of beginning again. He is a God of second chances and He cares for you.

Phyllis and I realize that we really own nothing in this life. We're just stewards of some things that God has given us. It's not our home; it's His home. It is filled with His love, His furniture, His appliances. If something breaks down, we let Him worry about it, because He supplies our every need. Jesus is everything.

In writing this book, it was extremely difficult for me to talk about my past life. You see, in God's sight it has all been done away with. My sins were not only forgiven, they were forgotten. As far as the east is from the west, that far has God removed our transgressions from us (Psalms 103:12). I praise Him daily for this assurance.

But I've had to live with my past, most of which was very, very unpleasant. It was hard for me to dig into my past because everything back there is just dung. I only really came alive in 1969. Since then my new life has been so exciting that I hated to relive any of the old life.

I share it in this book for one reason only. Here it is: *What God did for me, He will do for you.* Perhaps you're going down one of the roads I've already been down. Maybe you've experienced problems in one of the areas that I had trouble in. If so, you can see by now that Jesus Christ is your only answer. You need to accept Him as your personal Savior and Lord. Or, if you already have done that, you need to turn your whole life over to Him. God doesn't just want your name on a church roll. He wants you—your very life! He wants you to walk for Him, to talk for Him, to fish for other men and women.

If you are unsaved, you'll find here on the last page of this book a very simple sinner's prayer that you can pray, believing, and ask for Christ to come into your heart. He will save you, and He will perform the same miracle in your heart and life that He performed in mine—the miracle of new birth.

Jesus said, "Except a man be born again, he cannot see the kingdom of God" (John 3:3). And again He offered, "I am come that you might have life and that you might have it more abundantly" (John 10:10). Are you now experiencing the abundant life? Accept Jesus, and you will. Your whole world will be new.

You can read other books, you can travel the world searching, but you will still face the same old problem—the heavy burden of the lonely you. That is what you need to get away from—yourself, not God!

I escaped the old Richard Coss and found a new life in Christ. If a slum kid from Minneapolis can do it, so can you!

Phyllis and I would like to hear from you. We are available for revival meetings, speaking engagements, prison ministry workshops, motivational seminars, etc. We can be reached at the following address and phone number:

Richard and Phyllis Coss
P.O. Box 2154
Gulf Shores, Alabama 36542
(334) 948-4210

CHAPTER 16

The Oklahoma City Bombing

April 19, 1995 turned out to be the worst day of my life. I was in Kansas to preach at a Baptist church. I was staying with my friend, Pastor Gary Stanton. Gary had been a biker for many years and rode with the Hell's Angels and the Outlaws. He was converted to Christ in 1982 and several years later went to seminary and studied for the ministry. I had met Gary shortly after he was saved and he has been one of my good friends ever since.

On Wednesday morning, April 19, I had just stepped out of the shower and was getting dressed when Gary hollered upstairs, "Richard, you need to come down and watch television. Something bad has just happened in Oklahoma City. It's on every channel."

I asked, "Where in Oklahoma City?"

Gary said, "Downtown. A bomb or something just exploded in the downtown area and it's really bad. A lot of people are feared dead."

As I came down the stairs, I thought to myself, I have a lot of family in downtown Oklahoma City. My daughter, Edye, works for the Internal Revenue Service. Her two babies—my grandchildren, three-year-old Chase and two-year-old Colton—are in America's Kids Daycare Center. My son's wife, Kathy Coss, has her office in the Justice Building downtown. I thought to myself, surely my family is okay.

I sat down with Gary in the living room and began to watch

Chase (two years) and Colton (five months).

what would unfold as America's worst tragedy. My heart sank deep within me as we saw the wounded and bleeding people being helped to waiting ambulances and rescue stations. Many people were lying on the ground being tended to and we watched as the dead were being carried off. Dark smoke was billowing upwards—many cars parked in the area were still on fire. What a horrible, horrible mess, I thought to myself. What could have happened here?

Then, all of a sudden, the television camera zoomed in on a young redheaded girl. It was my daughter, Edye! And Edye was screaming, "Where are my babies? Has anybody seen my babies?"

My heart sank even deeper within me. Oh, my God—we're in trouble, I thought to myself. My next reaction was to grab the telephone and call Oklahoma City, but all of the phone lines were jammed. I prayed and said, "God, I must get through—help me get through to my family. Please, God."

That still, small voice of God came through and said, "Call your son." At that time, my son, Danny, was a police officer with the Yukon, Oklahoma police department. I picked up the telephone again and dialed the number of the Yukon police station.

The phone rang twice and a dispatcher answered. "Thank you, Jesus," I said under my breath. Then I told the dispatcher who I was and that I needed to talk to my son.

Danny had already been sent to downtown Oklahoma City to aid in the rescue work. The Yukon Police Department called my son on his cell phone and gave him my number. Danny immediately called me back. When I answered the phone, he said, "Dad, get home. It's real bad."

"Is it the boys?" I asked.

"Yes, Daddy, they're dead."

My son found and identified his own nephews, Chase and Colton, at the bombsite. Danny said to me on the phone, "Dad, how do I tell my sister her children are dead?"

I immediately packed my clothes and took off for Oklahoma City. As I drove to be with my family, I had a little over three hours to pray to God, reflect, and listen to that still, small voice of the Almighty Creator, Jesus Christ. The voice said, "You and Phyllis will be strong. I will make you strong. You both will be strength to your family and help them get through this trial. Richard, you will do your grandsons' funeral and I will strengthen you and give you the words that you will need to say. Put your trust in Me."

"Yes, Lord, who else? Only You and Your grace, mercy, and love can get us through this tragedy."

As I was nearing Oklahoma City, Phyllis had caught a flight out of Pensacola, Florida and God had spoken the same message to her: "I will make you strong—you will be strength to your family."

For the next ten days, we were constantly with our family members, praying for them and crying with them. Buckets full of tears must have been shed by all of us those first five or six days and there were lots of hugs going around. Ten days after the bombing we were able to put our little babies' bodies to rest. God did give me the strength and the words to preach my grandsons' funeral.

Edye said to me after the boys' homegoing, "Daddy, my boys are safe in Jesus. They can never be hurt again. Daddy, you will never have to visit your grandsons in jail. They will never be drug addicts or alcoholics and the child molesters can never hurt them. They're safe, Daddy. My boys are dancing before the Lord."

And how true that is. The word of God says "to be absent from this body is to be present with the Lord." Plus, we who are saved by the blood of Jesus get to see them again. Amen. God has a special way of turning "tragedy into triumph" and He has been at work in all of our lives.

Prior to the bombing, Edye had been divorced from her husband. Then came that awful moment, April 19, 1995, 9:00 A.M., and Edye and her ex-husband, the father of Chase and Colton, were brought back together because of the boys' death. They later decided to remarry.

But their marriage only lasted a short while and they divorced for the second time. How my heart was breaking for Edye. Only twenty-three years old and she had gone through so much.

Edye, Glenn, and Paul Stowe.

We kept praying. Jesus Christ is in the business of rebuilding broken hearts and ruined lives and He was working on all of us. Edye met Paul Stowe, a young man our family fell in love with. And I guess she fell in love with him also, because Dad performed a marriage ceremony.

On January 12, 1998, Edye gave birth to Glenn Brennon Stowe, seven pounds ten ounces and twenty-one inches long. What a difference a baby makes, especially in this family. In August prior to the birth, Edye had an ultrasound done and she called me and said, "Daddy, it's a boy. I needed a boy."

Glenn is the latest of our grandchildren and a great joy to Phyllis and me. Rom. 8:28 says, "For we know that all things work together for good to them who love the Lord and are called according to His purposes." Thank you, Lord, for Your promises. For Paul, Edye, and Glenn, life is just beginning.

RAP SHEET

Subject Richard David Coss—white male—height 5'11"— weight 190 lb.—hair, red—eyes, blue—Date of Birth 7/19/44. Identifying marks—tattoo, left wrist—FBI No. A2 33476SW

Record of Arrests

1957 Webster, Wisconsin—Breaking & entering, shoplifting, disobeying all authority. Subject 12 years old, sent to Madison Diagnostic Center, Madison, Wisconsin, 6 weeks, for diagnostic evaluation. Recommendation for probation and possible foster home placement.

1957 Bloomer, Wisconsin—Probation violation. County jail, 28 days.

1957 Waukesha, Wisconsin—Subject sent to State Training School for Boys, 18 months.

1959 Minneapolis, Minnesota—Expelled from school.

1960 Minneapolis, Minnesota—Driving without a license. 30 days—suspended.

1960 Minneapolis, Minnesota—Driving without a license. 30 days at county workhouse.

1960 Driving while intoxicated. 60 days at county workhouse.

1960	Minneapolis, Minnesota—driving without a license. 90 days at county workhouse.
6/10/61	Albuquerque, New Mexico—Suspicion robbery. Lie detector test. (No charges.)
1963	St. Cloud, Minnesota—Worthless checks. 30 days— suspended.
1963	Minneapolis, Minnesota—Assault. 30 days at county workhouse.
1964	Minneapolis, Minnesota—Assault & battery. 60 days at county workhouse.
3/25/65	Appeared in court in St. Cloud, Minnesota on Stearns County warrant. Worthless check.
4/13/65	St. Cloud, Minnesota—Worthless Check. 90 days— suspended and one year probation.
6/21/66	Omaha, Nebraska—Suspicion auto theft. (No Charges.)
6/26/66	Omaha, Nebraska—Suspicion theft, selling stolen property. (No charges.)
9/7/66	Minneapolis, Minnesota—Theft, auto; selling stolen cars (31 counts), reduced to theft. One year probation, four months county jail time.
9/7/66	Assaulting a police officer. (No charges.)
9/7/66	Concealed weapon (revolver). (No charges.)
9/7/66	Worthless check. 30 days concurrent with above jail time.
10/18/66	Warrant from Benton County (Minnesota) Sheriff. Disposing of property with a Mechanics Lien served on subject. County jail 25 days.
12/19/66	St. Cloud, Minnesota—Hold on warrant from 1963. Defeating Security on Personality. 30 days county jail.
3/6/67	Minneapolis, Minnesota—Probation violation, warrant filed, whereabouts unknown.
3/19/67	Juarez, Mexico—Selling stolen auto. Hold at Chihuahua State Prison for deportation.

5/16/67	El Paso, Texas—For Dyer Act, a Hold placed warrant for probation violation.
5/31/67	El Paso, Texas—Subject committed to Federal Bureau of Prisons. 4 years on Dyer Act, El Reno, Oklahoma. Served 18 months.
6/19/67	Minneapolis, Minnesota—Probation violation concurrent with federal sentence. Other warrants released.
10/24/67	District Court Commitment. Workhouse, 1 year.
10/25/67	Subject in custody El Reno, Oklahoma Prison on Dyer Act, Auto Theft.
9/30/68	Oklahoma City, Oklahoma—Dyer Act; Miami, Florida to Oklahoma City. Three years consecutive with balance 4-year sentence.
10/3/68	Oklahoma City, Oklahoma—Dyer Act; Oklahoma City to Wichita, Kansas. Three years consecutive with 9/30/68 3-year sentence. Returned to El Reno Federal Reformatory. Served 2 more years.

RAP SHEET

Subject	Phyllis L. Coss. Alias: Phyllis L. Holt, Phyllis Louise Craft, Phyllis Johnson, Phyllis L. Shaw, Phyllis McCaslin—Tulsa County, Oklahoma.

Record of Arrests

7/7/60	Tulsa, Oklahoma—Vagrancy. Dismissed.
7/12/60	Tulsa, Oklahoma—Vagrancy. Dismissed.
1/20/61	Tulsa, Oklahoma—Public drunk. Dismissed.
2/10/61	Tulsa, Oklahoma—Assault and battery. 10 days
5/22/61	Tulsa, Oklahoma—Public drunk. 30 days.
7/2/61	Tulsa, Oklahoma—Shoplifting. 30 days.

10/11/61	Tulsa, Oklahoma—Shoplifting. 28 days.
3/30/62	Tulsa, Oklahoma—Assault and battery. Dismissed.
6/8/62	U.S. Postal Money Order fraud. 3 years federal probation.
11/13/65	Tulsa, Oklahoma—Negligent homicide. 1 year probation
7/5/66	Alderson, West Virginia—Passing counterfeit money. 10 years federal prison; served 6 months.
9/8/68	Tulsa, Oklahoma—Stolen vehicle. 60 days.
2/10/69	Tulsa, Oklahoma—Public drunk. Dismissed.
5/24/69	Alderson, West Virginia—Counterfeit money. Served 27 months federal prison.
1/17/73	Tulsa, Oklahoma—Larceny. 30 days.
1/17/73	Tulsa, Oklahoma—Larceny. 30 days concurrent.
3/16/73	Tulsa, Oklahoma—Receiving stolen property. 30 days.
7/12/74	Tulsa, Oklahoma—Larceny. Paid fine.

At the time this book was being written, Phyllis applied for a Presidential Pardon.

"A SINNER'S PRAYER"

Dear Father, I come to you in Jesus' name and I ask you to forgive me of my sins and to come into my life and take over every part of me.

Jesus, fill my life with your Holy Spirit that others might see YOU in me.

Satan and demons, I rebuke your evil work in and around my life forever.

Thank you, Lord. In Jesus' name I pray. Amen.

Glory, Hallelujah!